COURTYARD, BAZAAR, TEMPLE

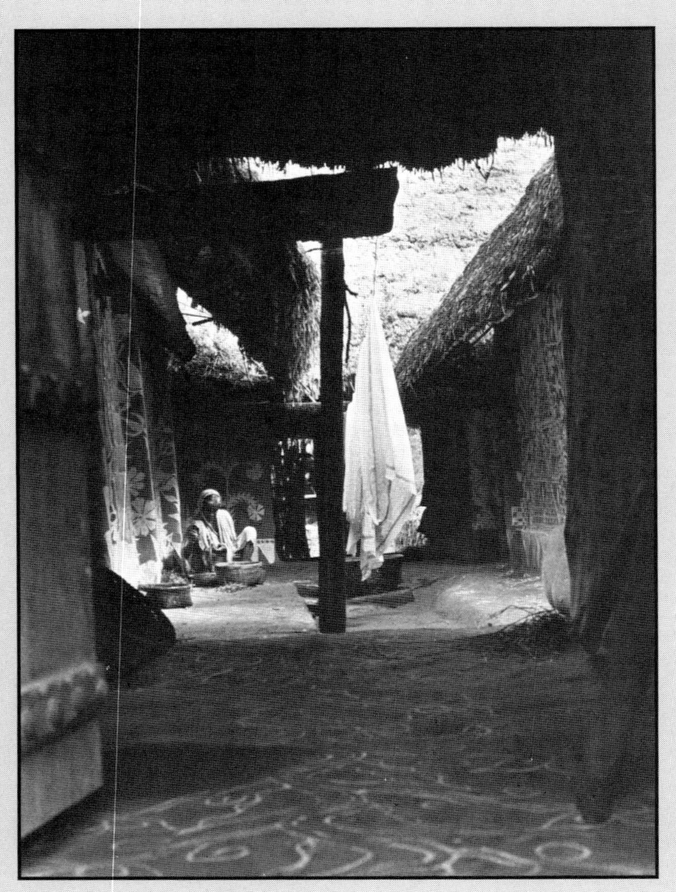

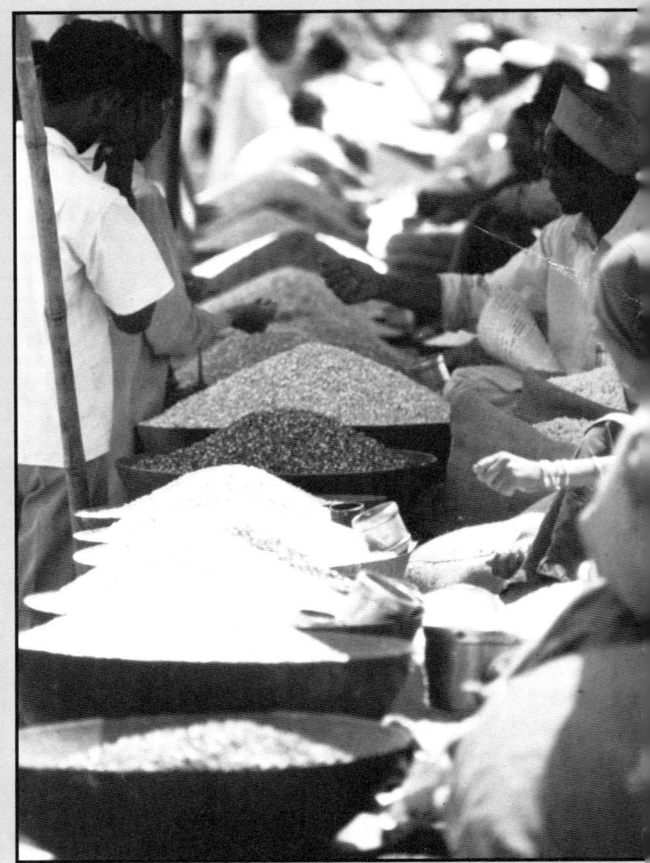

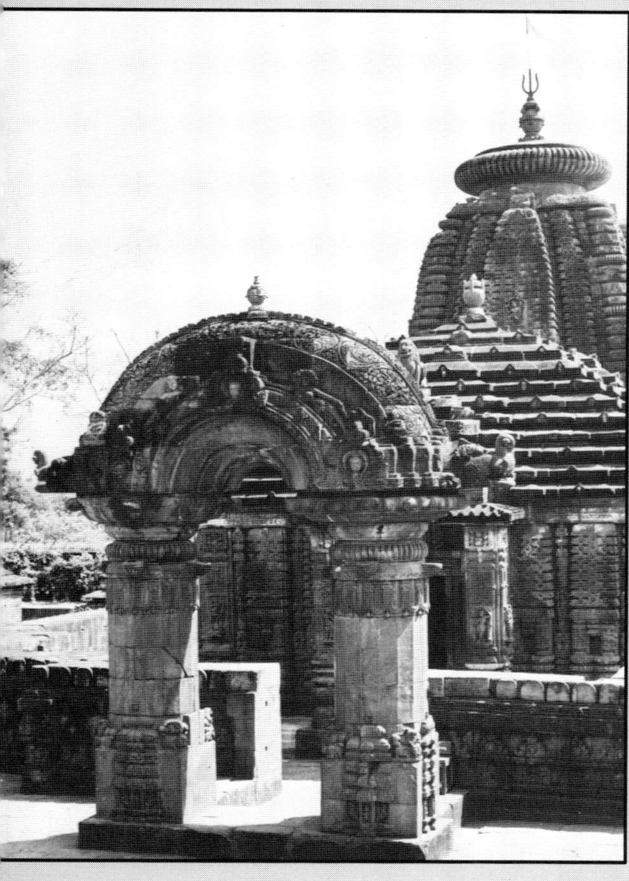

COURTYARD, BAZAAR, TEMPLE: TRADITIONS OF TEXTILE EXPRESSION IN INDIA

An exhibition organized by the
Costume and Textile Study Center,
University of Washington, Seattle

by Katherine F. Hacker
and Krista Jensen Turnbull

Courtyard, Bazaar, Temple: Traditions of Textile Expression in India was organized by the Costume and Textile Study Center at the University of Washington and is being published in connection with an exhibition at the Bellevue Art Museum, Bellevue, Washington, 12 June–25 July 1982.

Printed in the United States of America
Distributed by the University of Washington Press

This project is funded by a grant from the National Endowment for the Humanities in Washington, D.C., a federal agency.

Cataloging in Publication Data

Hacker, Katherine F.
Courtyard, bazaar, temple: traditions of textile expression in India.

1. Textile fabrics—India—Catalogs. 2. Costume—India—Catalogs. 3. India—Social life and customs. I. Turnbull, Krista Jensen. II. Bellevue Art Museum. III. Title.

NK 8976 H33 746.1

ISBN 0-295-95966-5
LC 82-50077

Textiles from the Collections housed at the University of Washington include accession numbers. Length precedes width in all measurements, which are noted in yards and inches. Metric measurements are in parentheses.

Cover photograph: ***Odhani*** *(head covering), Saurashtra, Gujarat, early 20th century. Silk; woven, satin weave; resist-dyed; printed, hand blocked with wax or paste resist; indigo dyed; 4 yd. 11 in. (3.95m) x 1 yd. 14 in. (1.27m); 58.2-82.*

Acknowledgments

This exhibition and catalogue are the realization of a project that began twenty years ago when Elizabeth Bayley Willis collected textiles in India. The anticipated outcome was a published record of her collection. Although a few of these textiles have been displayed in the past, this exhibition is the first major showing. This project was made possible by a generous grant from the National Endowment for the Humanities.

The South Asia Studies Program of the School of International Studies at the University of Washington, as cosponsors of the project, has greatly contributed to its success. Pat Emerson, Outreach Coordinator, and Frank Conlon, Associate Professor, South Asia Studies and History, have provided input and support since the project's inception. Richard Salomon, Assistant Professor, Asian Languages and Literature and South Asia Studies, translated Oriya on one of the Orissan textiles into Sanskrit and English. Michael Shapiro, Associate Professor, Asian Languages and Literature and South Asia Studies, assisted in standardizing the spelling of terms for our glossary. Professors Dan Neuman, Lorraine Sakata, Frank Conlon, Jack Hawley, Michael Shapiro, Richard Salomon, and Aurora Valentinetti presented lectures to more fully develop the humanities themes of the exhibition. Ustad Sabri Khan, University of Washington visiting artist-in-residence, Ghulam Sarwar, and Ratna Roy of the Urvasi Dance Troupe greatly enhanced this varied program. Irene Joshi, South Asia Librarian, organized a display of rare books for the Suzzallo Library Rotunda, University of Washington campus, to compliment our exhibition.

John Olbrantz, Director of the Bellevue Art Museum, not only provided space for the exhibition but also financial and staff support. Convergence '82, a committee of Handweavers Guild of America, in recognition of the Costume and Textile Study Center as a valuable community resource, provided additional financial support for the catalogue. Our research assistants, Maureen McFarland and Susan Torntore, each contributed their energies, talents, and enthusiasm to the project. Vicki Adams, our editor, and Rick Koppes, our designer, have worked closely with all written and visual materials and contributed to the success of the project. Elizabeth Frenz volunteered countless hours preparing textiles for exhibition. Martha Fletcher mounted the patola fragments and Rajasthani turban fragments for exhibition. Gary McFarland produced, edited, and distributed a public service announcement on the exhibition to assure a much wider audience.

This exhibition has provided an excellent opportunity to show more of the Costume and Textile Study Center's extensive holdings. In addition to the Willis Collection, textiles from Mrs. Russell J. Matthias, Mrs. Helen Stager Poulsen, the Harriet Tidball Collection, and the Garbaty Collection were exhibited.

While developing themes for the exhibition, we found it necessary to borrow from other institutions. Mrs. Willis' textiles are also housed at the Museum of Natural History of the Smithsonian Institution. They provided a *telia rumal* from her collection. The Lowie Museum of Anthropology, University of California, Berkeley; The UCLA Museum of Cultural History, Los Angeles; and the Seattle Art Museum provided important artifacts. Private collections were also utilized and we wish to thank Mr. and Mrs. Jermeja Singh Hundal, Gyöngy Laky, Mrs. Sarala Sharma, Leslie Grace of Folk Art Gallery/La Tienda, and Ron Granich of Cerulean Blue.

The majority of the field photographs are from the collection of Katherine and Bill Hacker; Susan Torntore provided most of the studio photographs. We also wish to thank Niranjan B. Benegal and Howard Giske of Seattle, Eberhard Fischer, Zurich, and the Santa Barbara Museum of Art, California, for providing additional photographs for the catalogue and poster.

Material in the catalogue was researched in India, in 1978-79, by Katherine Hacker. This research was made possible by a Fulbright-Hayes Grant sponsored by the All India Handloom Board. C. S. Ramakrishnan, Director, United States Educational Foundation in India, New Delhi; A. V. Ramamurthy, Director, Indian Institute of Handloom Technology, Varanasi; and Vijayan Puliampet, India Director, Berkeley Professional Studies Program, greatly facilitated field work in weaving centers and villages throughout India. A special thank you is extended to friends and colleagues in India whose warmth, hospitality, and willingness to share made work very rewarding.

Most importantly, we acknowledge the craftspeople of India whose skills have produced the beautiful textiles we have the opportunity to present in this exhibition and catalogue.

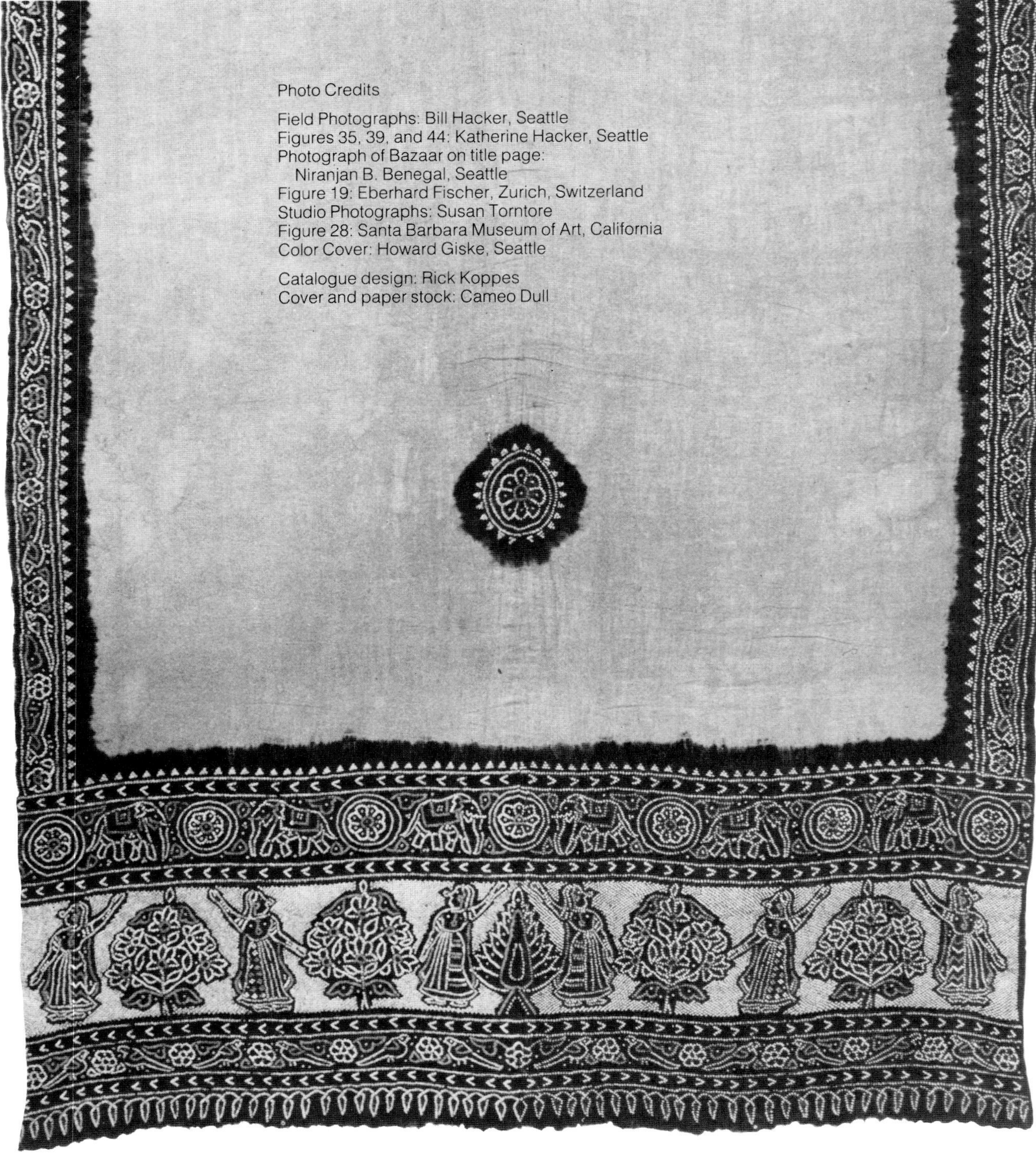

Photo Credits

Field Photographs: Bill Hacker, Seattle
Figures 35, 39, and 44: Katherine Hacker, Seattle
Photograph of Bazaar on title page:
Niranjan B. Benegal, Seattle
Figure 19: Eberhard Fischer, Zurich, Switzerland
Studio Photographs: Susan Torntore
Figure 28: Santa Barbara Museum of Art, California
Color Cover: Howard Giske, Seattle

Catalogue design: Rick Koppes
Cover and paper stock: Cameo Dull

Contents

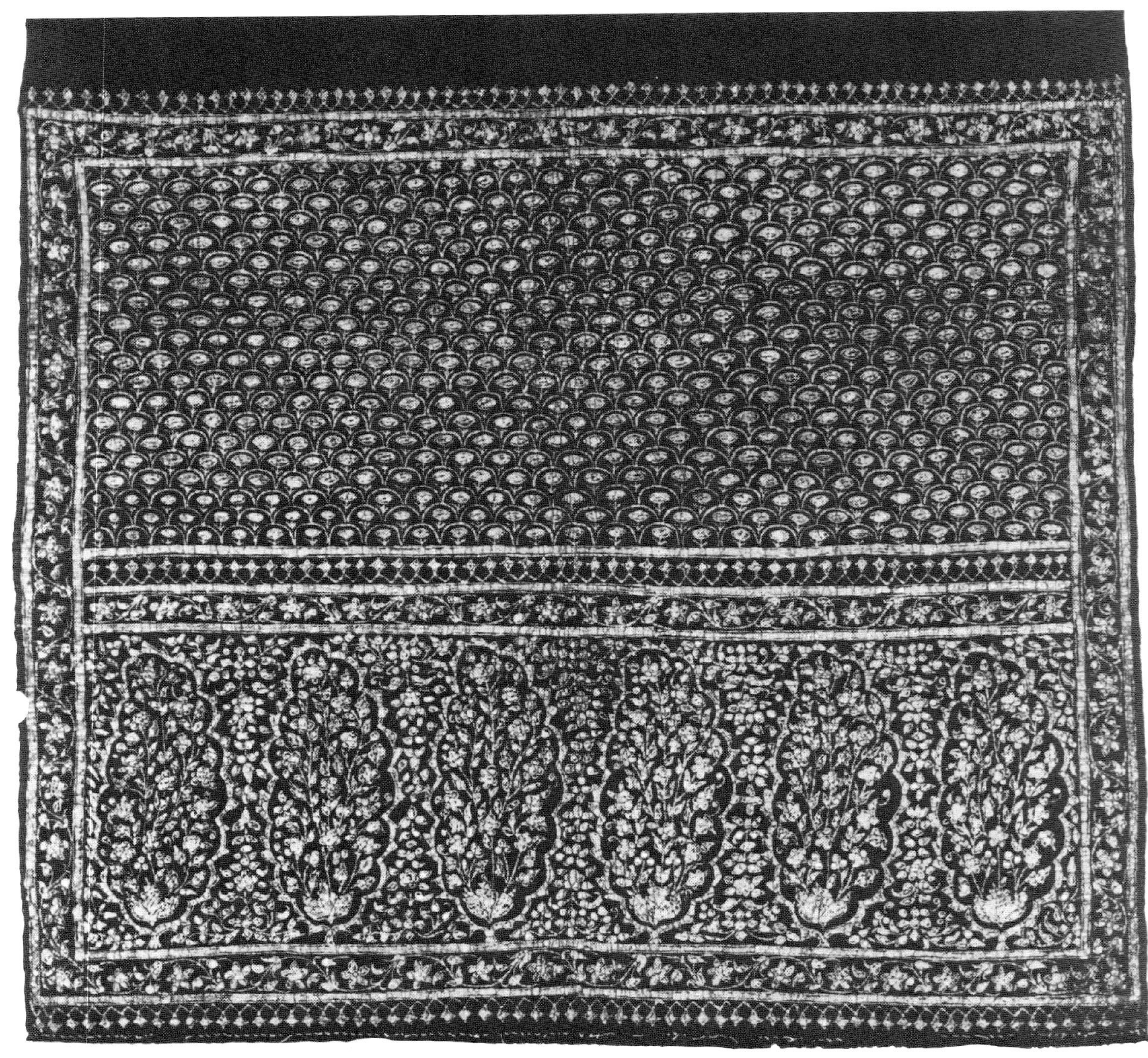

Fig. 1. Detail of **patka** *(ceremonial sash), Rajasthan or Gujarat, 19th century. Cotton; woven; indigo dyed; hand printed, stenciled (tinsel printed), application of silver, gold, and beetle wings; 1 yd. 34 in. (1.78m) × 25¾ in. (.65m); 58.2-91.*

The Elizabeth Bayley Willis Collection

In 1958 the University of Washington received from Virginia and Prentice Bloedel of Bainbridge Island, Washington, the very generous gift of the Elizabeth Bayley Willis Collection of textiles from India. The initial collection has been added to over the years by Mrs. Willis and the Bloedels. The collection, which consists of over 1,400 artifacts from South Asia, includes handwoven, embroidered, printed, resist dyed, and painted textiles, weaving tools, jewelry, and dolls. The primary focus of the collection is India. The majority of these textiles are *saris* and were contemporary when they were purchased from the weavers and craftsmen at the time of production from 1952 through 1964. Textiles from over one hundred and fifty cities, towns and villages, and weaving centers in India are represented; textiles from neighboring Bangladesh, Bhutan, Sikkim, Tibet, Burma, and Pakistan are also included.

Under British colonial rule in the nineteenth century, India's markets were flooded with inexpensive machine-made fabrics from Britain. The indigenous textile heritage was in danger of disappearing. Mahatma Gandhi chose textiles as a symbol of resurgent Indian national pride and purpose, invoking a concern for the preservation of all that was good in their society, their culture and their textiles. It was in this setting that Elizabeth Bayley Willis first went to India.

In 1952 the government of India established the All India Handicrafts Board, the All India Handloom Board, and the Khadi and Village Industries Board. The goals were twofold: to improve and develop crafts production, and to promote sales in India and abroad, thereby enhancing the living and working conditions of the craftsmen. The government of Uttar Pradesh contacted the United Nations Technical Assistance Board asking for a foreign adviser to aid in preservation, development, and export of cottage and small hand industry products. Mrs. Willis was recommended as a person qualified in museum work with a strong background in decorative arts and marketing. As Technical Adviser on Handicraft Development, she spent a year traveling to villages and production sites of Uttar Pradesh working with the craftsmen and developing export markets. Mrs. Willis states that "while working in India, I realized the great and very special privilege of working among craftsmen and finding examples of techniques and designs which were often unique and one of a kind." As a response to this sense of specialness, she began her own collection.

In 1955 Mrs. Willis was recalled to India to serve as a Gazetted Officer and was adviser to the Ministry of Commerce and Industry, the Textile Commissioner, and the All India Handloom Board. Her role was to develop the export business for handloom textiles for all of India. For the next two years, she visited hundreds of villages and towns where handloom textiles were produced. Working closely with government officials, she helped establish guidelines for quality controls and technical improvements. As she worked with the weavers, she also purchased examples of their work and examples of historic textiles. Following this two-year assignment, Mrs. Willis returned to India as a tourist several times between 1957 and 1964. She continued her research on the textile industry in an attempt to document this rapidly changing art.

In 1958, as Mrs. Willis was at her home documenting hundreds of textiles from India, she was visited by her long time friend, Virginia Bloedel. Mrs. Willis' intent was to offer the collection to a museum on the east coast. Mrs. Bloedel felt strongly that this valuable resource should stay in the Pacific Northwest. The Bloedels, generous benefactors to the University of Washington for many years, offered to buy the collection and give it to the University.

This major gift was the start of the Costume and Textile Study Center. This facility now houses one of the finest textile collections in the United States. Approximately 11,000 textiles comprise examples of all the textile arts. Included are ethnic and historic costume, functional and decorative textiles, as well as ornamental objects and implements used in the production of textiles. In addition, an extensive research library includes three thousand books, and other publications on textiles. As part of the School of Nutritional Sciences and Textiles, this facility serves the university community and the public as a research center for those interested in textile research.

This catalogue and exhibition are dedicated to Elizabeth Bayley Willis in recognition and appreciation of her significant collection of Indian textiles.

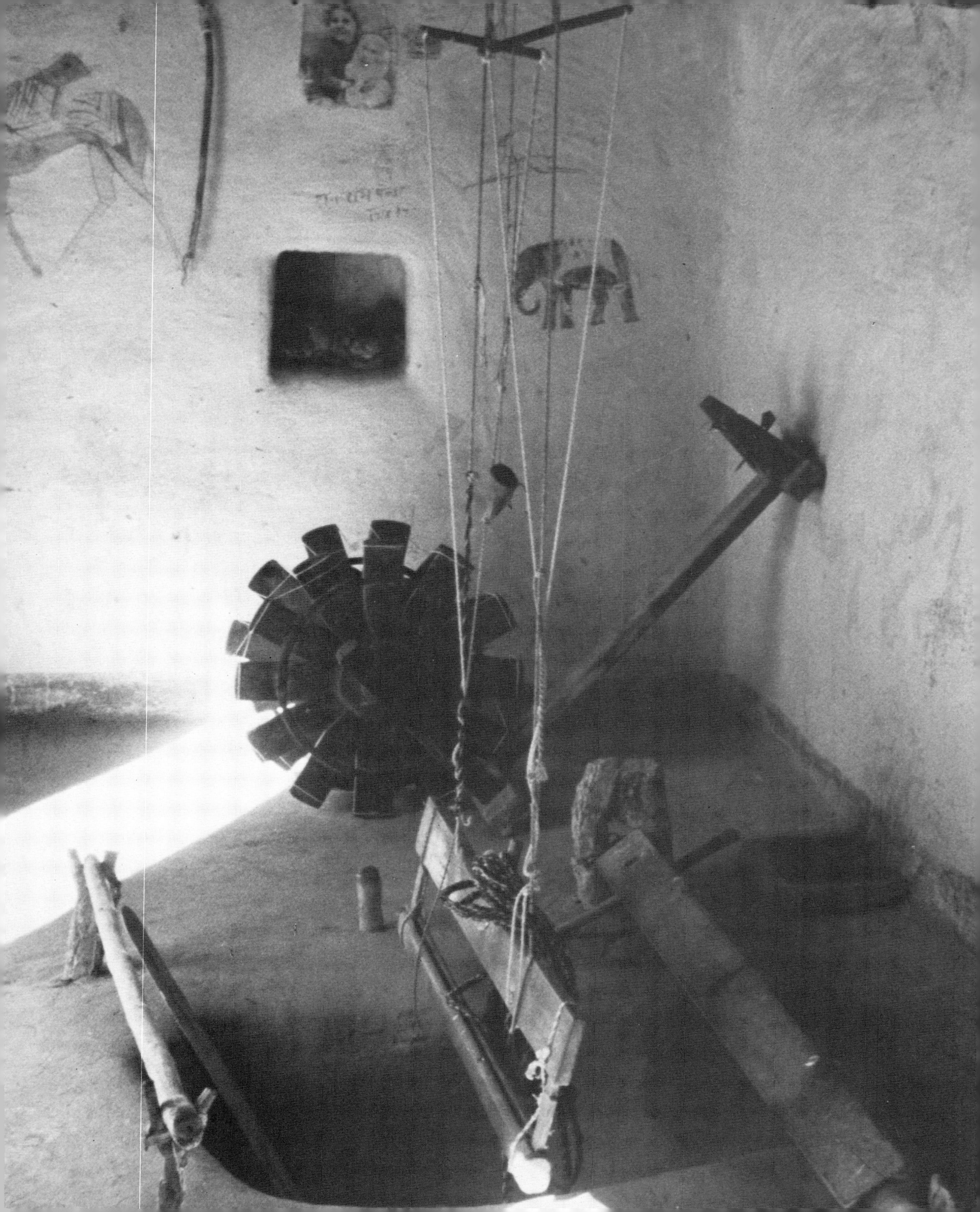

TEXTILES OF INDIA

Throughout the history of India and continuing today is a great and diverse textile heritage that enriches all aspects of life. From the days of cotton cultivation in the ancient Indus Valley to Mahatma Gandhi's choice of textiles as a symbol of Indian national pride, textiles have played a significant role in India's culture. To better understand the significance of textiles in India, one must see them as part of the larger contexts where they are made and used. The courtyard, bazaar, and temple symbolize these contexts. They provide the domestic, social, and religious frameworks that give meaning and order to the existence of India's people. Each represents a different level of social interchange, none of which is exclusive. Their interrelationship is extremely complex, with each reinforcing the other to build and maintain cultural stability. This rich textile heritage continues today primarily in the villages where approximately 80 percent of India's people live.

The courtyard, a common feature of the Indian village house, expresses an Indian preference for living and working outside. Throughout the country, the courtyard and its placement in the house differ as shown in Map 1, but it remains the focal point of family life. Numerous activities occur in the courtyard, not only weaving and the preparation of materials for weaving, but also winnowing of grains, preparing fodder for animals, and talking to neighbors. Prominently placed in the plan of the house is the pit loom, the most widely used loom in India (Fig. 2). This counterbalance treadle loom is grounded, which gives it great stability yet limits the width of its cloth. The products of the loom are primarily articles of clothing and clearly demonstrate loom restrictions and capabilities.

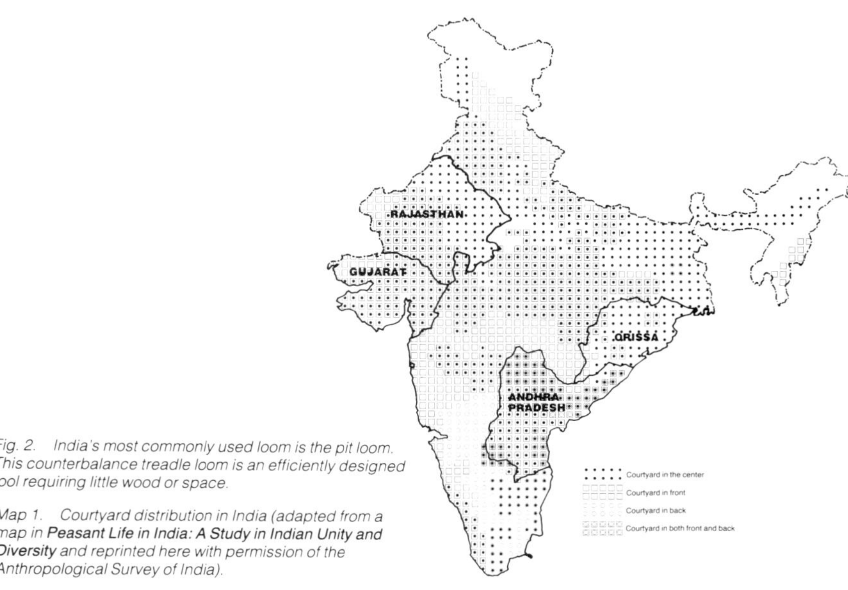

Fig. 2. India's most commonly used loom is the pit loom. This counterbalance treadle loom is an efficiently designed tool requiring little wood or space.

Map 1. Courtyard distribution in India (adapted from a map in ***Peasant Life in India: A Study in Indian Unity and Diversity*** *and reprinted here with permission of the Anthropological Survey of India).*

In the bazaar, trade, economy, and the bonds of caste are often prescribed by thousands of years of cultural history. Caste dictated occupations, and a natural outgrowth of this was homogeneous skill communities and workshops still apparent in the bazaars of India's cities today. Separate areas of the bazaar are devoted to the display of different goods, including textiles, jewelry, brassware, and food. Textiles, densely displayed in the shops, extend out into the street and contribute to the color, richness, and vitality of the bazaars.

In the temple, each Indian faces the most intimate interchange of all, that between God and Man. The temples, physical and visual symbols of the religious teaching of Hinduism, outwardly convey the tenets of religion through the sculptured reliefs and friezes that lavishly adorn the exteriors. Temple cloths perform that same function in the interior. This visual presentation is of vital importance in the preservation of the religious tradition of India, especially among unlettered villagers.

The integrity of the traditions of textile expression in India has been assured by the caste and family structures. India's craftsmen work within a set of conditions predetermined by caste. This static hierarchical system has historically bound people to specific occupations. The extended family, with generations of skills within one household, further contributes to the continuity and distinct regional character of textile expression.

The Regional Diversity of Textiles

In addition to cultural factors, the economy, geography, climate, technology, and material availability all contribute to a distinctive regional textile expression. Textiles have always played a primary role in the Indian economy, where they currently comprise the second largest industry surpassed only by agriculture.

The physical characteristics of India present a diverse landscape: great tracts of desert in the west, chains of mountains north to south, and major river systems. The importance of the river cannot be overemphasized, and it has throughout time been regarded with reverence and devotion. Many of India's cities developed from pilgrimage centers located on rivers. Rivers continue to support her cities and villages alike.

Materials available for the tools and fibers used in weaving vary from region to region. Wood and space, both at a premium in India, determine the regional construction of the pit loom. Cotton, readily available throughout India, is woven to produce everyday garments for both men and women and occasionally is combined with gold for special occasions. Wild silk, indigenous to India, is found along the eastern river systems—the Ganges, Godavari, Mahanadi, and Brahmaputra. Mulberry silk requires a cooler temperature and is only cultivated in higher elevations in India. Wool, camel, and goat hair are used in the production of textiles in the north and west including Kutch and the Thar desert.

Orissa, Andhra Pradesh, Rajasthan, and Gujarat, outlined in Map 2, are four of India's states that demonstrate cultural, material, and geographic diversity, while sharing common textile techniques. The selected emphasis in this catalogue is resist dyed, printed, and painted textiles from these four states. They are well represented in and parallel strengths of the Elizabeth Bayley Willis Collection. A long tradition of textile production and motif interpretation gives a regionality and cultural importance to the textiles of these four states.

Map 2. Geographic diversity in India. Outlines show the states of Orissa, Andhra Pradesh, Rajasthan, and Gujarat.

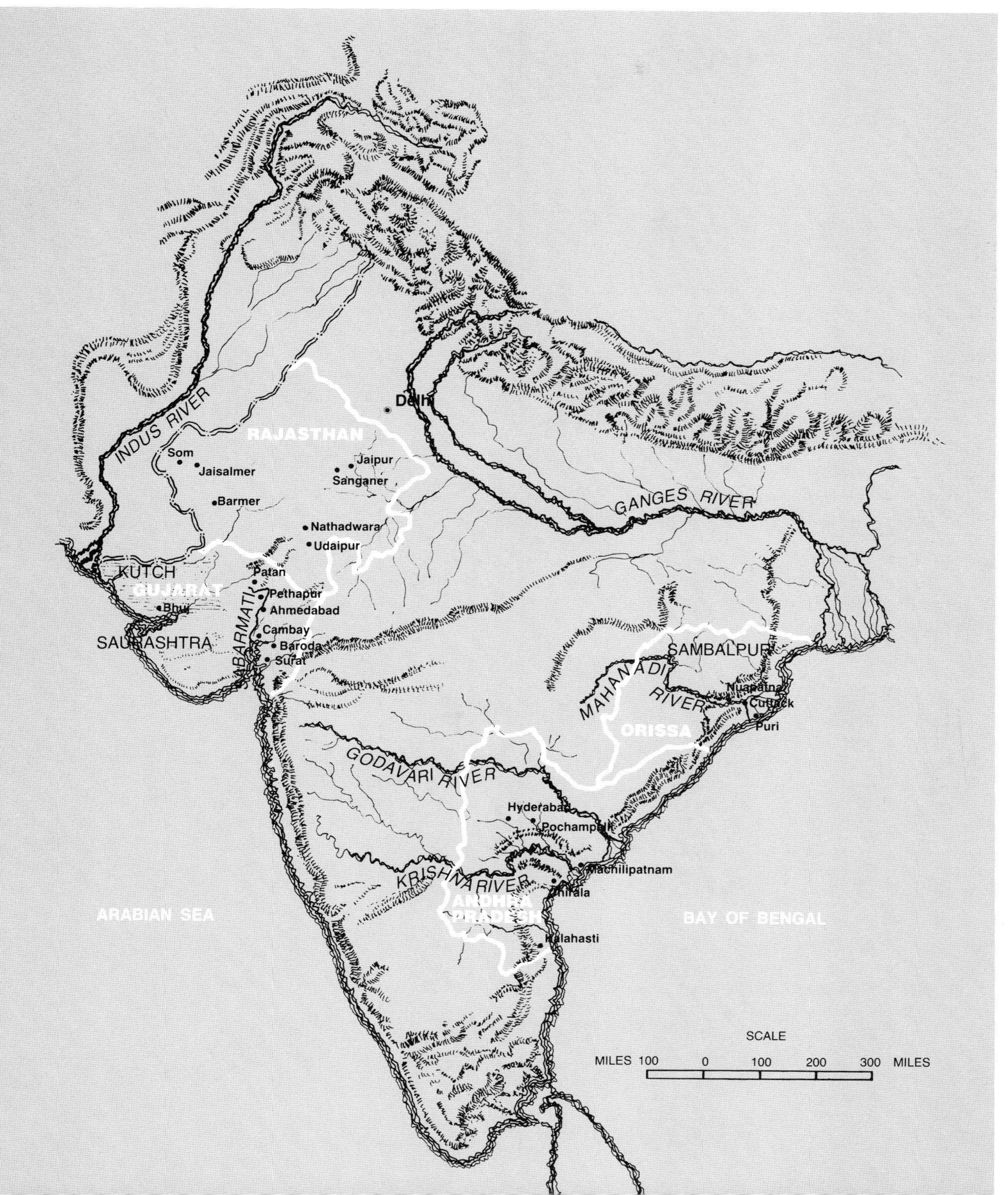
INDUS RIVER
Delhi
RAJASTHAN
Som
Jaisalmer
Jaipur
Sanganer
Barmer
Nathadwara
Udaipur
GANGES RIVER
KUTCH
Patan
GUJARAT
Pethapur
Ahmedabad
Bhuj
SAURASHTRA
Cambay
Baroda
Surat
SABARMATI
SAMBALPUR
MAHANADI RIVER
Nuapatna
Cuttack
Puri
ORISSA
GODAVARI RIVER
Hyderabad
Pochampalli
Machilipatnam
KRISHNA RIVER
Chirala
ANDHRA PRADESH
Kalahasti
ARABIAN SEA
BAY OF BENGAL
SCALE
MILES 100 0 100 200 300 MILES

Textiles as Clothing

Draped textiles are India's indigenous garments. They are deftly folded, pleated, and draped, and the style of drapery identifies the area of the country that the wearer is from as clearly as do regional motifs. The most common woman's garment, as shown in Map 3, is the *sari*, a rectangular piece of cloth the width of the loom (approximately 42 to 48 inches) and four to six yards long. The sari is distinguished by a decorative end two or three feet long known as the *pallu*. The patterning of the *pallu* compliments the design in the field and often repeats part of the border motifs. The *odhani*, a traditional woman's garment of northwest India, is worn as a headcovering. It is made from two equal lengths of loom-width cloth decoratively joined.

Men's traditional garments, like women's, are long pieces of cloth draped around the body. The *dhoti*, a man's lower garment made of a single length of cloth approximately four yards long, conveys a regionality in its style of drapery. The *lungi,* another lower garment, is shorter than the *dhoti* and wrapped and knotted around the waist with the extra cloth gathered and pleated in the front. The man's *dhabla* or *kambla,* a shoulder cloth or blanket, is the man's counterpart to the *odhani* and is produced on narrow looms in rural Rajasthan and Gujarat. The *pagri,* or turban, again communicates information concerning the wearer's village both in motif and in wrapping technique.

Stitched or constructed garments show the Muslim influence on clothing which began with the invasions of the eighth century. The distribution of their use, as shown in Map 3, is explained by the repeated invasions of the northwest. The *choli* is a short blouse worn with a sari or *ghaghara.* The *ghaghara,* or full skirt, worn by women of western India, is constructed in one of two ways. A length of up to twenty yards is gathered and attached to a waistband or the length of cloth is cut into gored panels and sewn. Other sewn garments are the *pyjama, salwar,* and *churi dar,* all trousers with drawstring waists. Each has a differently constructed leg. The *churi dar* and *salwar* are worn by men and women; the *salwar* is also known as *ejar* when it is worn with the *aba* by the Muslim women of Kutch, Gujarat. The *aba* is a tuniclike dress whose name has a Persian derivative meaning "an outer garment."

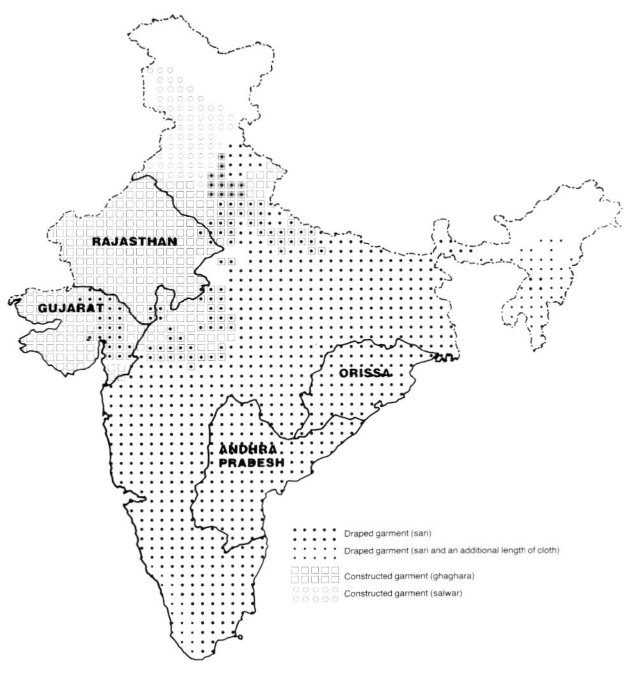

Map 3. Women's draped and constructed garments (adapted from a map in ***Peasant Life in India*** *and reprinted here with permission of the Anthropological Survey of India).*

Textiles as Religious Expression

Textiles not only clothe India's vast population of six hundred and fifty million but also play an important role in the religious expression of the people. In the Indian experience, religion is not simply a set of beliefs, but rather a comprehensive way of life. It is based not only on text but also relies on context, defining and shaping traditional values. In India, Hinduism, Jainism, Buddhism, and Islam all manifest this quality of religion as an all-embracing way of life. Religious motifs and depictions of gods are often incorporated into the patterns of clothing and household textiles. Often portrayed is the elephant-headed god, Ganesha, the son of Shiva and remover of obstacles. The *Ganesha Stha-*

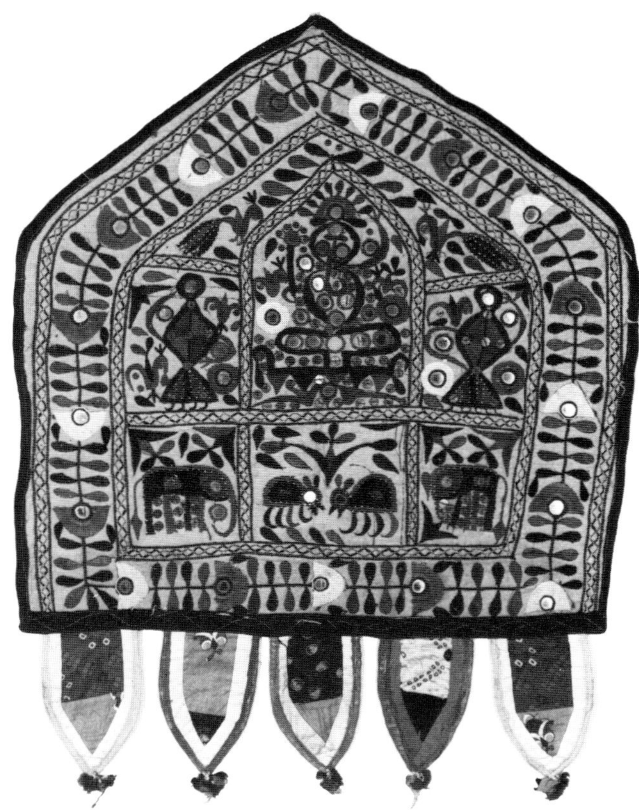

Fig. 3. ***Ganesha Sthapana*** (dowry piece), Saurashtra, Gujarat, 20th century. The bridal couple first make their offerings to ***Ganesha**, the elephant-headed god and bestower of good fortune, who is portrayed on this* ***sthapana.*** *The shape of the top of the textile resembles the gabled roof of a temple. Cotton; woven; printed; resist dyed,* **bandhana**; *embroidered, stitches: chain, herringbone (tied), buttonhole, cretan, herringbone (variation to attach shisha), cretan-herringbone; mirror embroidery; 26 in. (.66m) × 19 in. (.482m); 81.9-131. Gift of Helen Stager Poulsen, Oakland.*

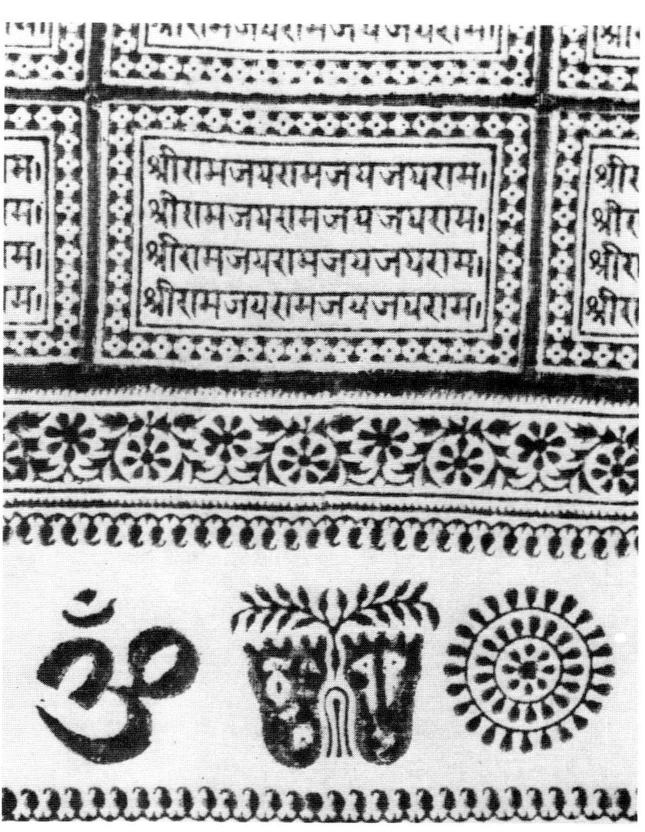

Fig. 4. ***Gamcha*** *(pilgrim's cloth), Varanasi, Uttar Pradesh, 20th century. Written in Devanagari script is the repeating invocation, "Shri Ram, Jai Ram, Jai Jai Ram." Cotton, woven; printed, hand blocked; 6 yd. 13 in. (5.83m) × 1 yd. 5 in. (1.04m); 58.2-78.*

pana, an embroidered and resist dyed textile, is one of a set of prescribed dowry textiles from Saurashtra, Gujarat (Fig. 3). In the immediate environment of the home, textiles serve as garments and decoration for the household deity and as coverings or containers for the ritually prescribed objects taken to the temple for *puja,* a religious ceremony. Textiles can also provide a visual record of a successful pilgrimage and are sold as a remembrance for the traveling pilgrims (Fig. 4).

Within the temple context, textiles are created not only as clothing for the gods but as temple cloths. In each of these four states a distinctive religious textile is produced that interprets the Great Tradition of Hinduism in a regional manner. The *"Gitagovinda"* cloth of Orissa is used in the worship of Jagannath, a manifestation of Krishna. Krishna is known as Shri Nathji by one sect in Rajasthan and his depiction is seen in the *pichhavai* temple cloth. The *kalamkari* temple cloth of Kalahasti, Andhra Pradesh, illustrates scenes from Hindu epics such as the *"Mahabharata"* and the *"Ramayana."* The *Mata Pachedi* of Gujarat is a temple cloth for the worship of the Mother Goddess in her many manifestations. Each textile conveys a specific message reflecting the vitality, power, and presence of religion in India.

Techniques of Textile Expression

Resist Dyeing

Resist dyeing involves the protecting or reserving of portions of fibers or fabrics from dye penetration to create designs or patterns. If the resisting process occurs only once, the pattern is monochromatic, while polychrome textiles are created by repeating the process.

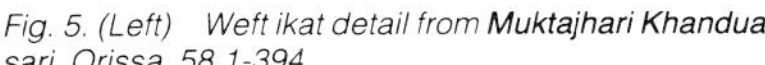

Fig. 5. (Left) Weft ikat detail from ***Muktajhari Khandua*** *sari, Orissa, 58.1-394.*

Fig. 6. (Center) ***Bandhana*** *detail from* ***pallu*** *of sari, early 20th century, 58.2-213.*

Fig. 7. (Right) Paste or wax resist detail from silk ***odhani,*** *Saurashtra, Gujarat, 58.2-82.*

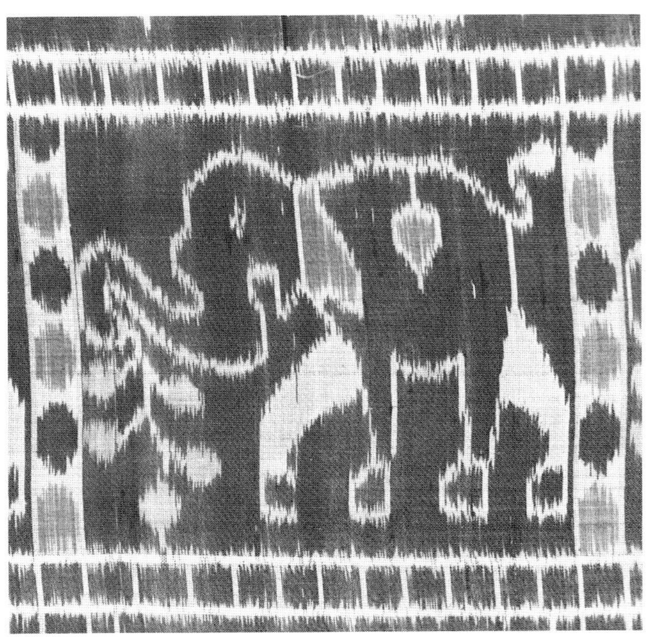

Ikat. In the resist dye process of ikat the *fibers* are resisted prior to dyeing and weaving. Areas to be resisted are tightly bound by hand with a variety of materials including cotton thread, palm leaf strips, bast fibers, and strips of plastic. If the warp threads are resisted and dyed prior to being placed under tension on the loom the resulting pattern is referred to as *warp ikat.* The weft threads, which are woven into alternating sheds of the warp to form a fabric, may also be resisted prior to weaving. If this occurs the pattern is a *weft ikat.* Often both the warp and weft are resisted and dyed prior to weaving, resulting in *double ikat* textiles where both elements join to create a preplanned pattern when woven. Characteristic of ikat resists are patterns with soft feathered outlines in either the warp or weft direction, depending on the yarn tied (Fig. 5).

In India today, ikat is practiced in Orissa, Andhra Pradesh, and Gujarat. In Orissa warp, weft, and double ikat techniques result in regionally distinctive saris and religious textiles of cotton and silk. Andhra Pradesh's weavers produce ikat saris and a specific regional clothing type, the ikat *telia rumal. Patola,* the double ikat silk textiles of Gujarat, demonstrate great technical mastery.

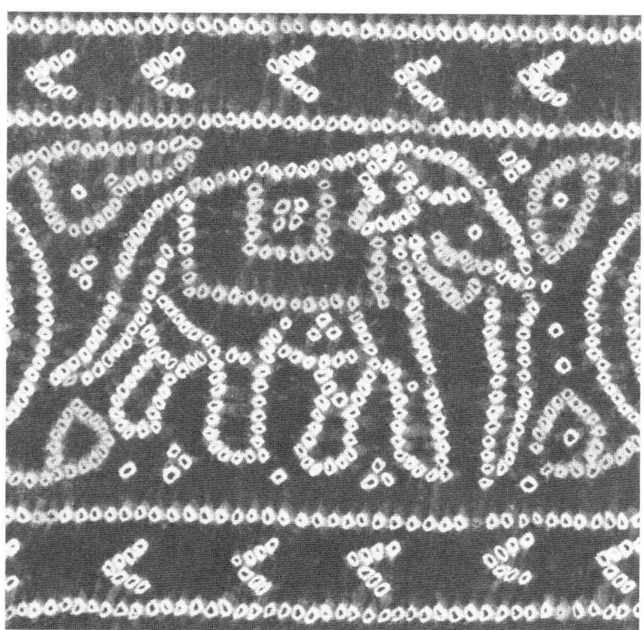

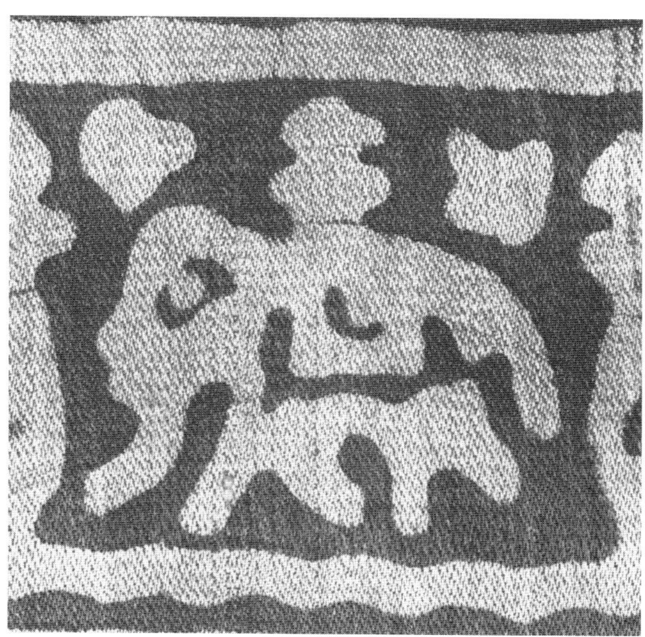

Bandhana. In the resist dyed process of *bandhana* the *fabric* is resisted prior to dyeing. The term *bandhana* is derived from the Hindi *bandhna* which means "to tie or bind." The Malay-Indonesian term for the *bandhana* technique of resist dyeing is *plangi.* (While *plangi* is often accepted as the primary term for the technique most commonly known as tie and dye, this catalogue will utilize the Indian *bandhana.*) Portions of the fabric to be reserved are raised and tightly resist-tied with threads or bast. The areas resisted create a negative pattern of dots after the dyeing and removal of the ties (Fig. 6). *Bandhana* is practiced extensively in the states of Rajasthan and Gujarat.

A resist dye technique belonging to the *bandhana* grouping is that of bound resist. The fabric to be resisted is rolled into a coil and sections of the fabric are tightly bound with thread or bast. Following the dye bath the fabric will have rows of dyed and undyed stripes. In the turbans of Rajasthan this process is often completed in both the warp and weft directions producing an overlapping plaid pattern, or on the bias producing diagonal stripes.

Application of a Resist. The second resist dye technique in which the *fabric* is resisted involves the application of a fluid or semifluid substance to the surface of the fabric. The Malay-Indonesian term for the application of wax resist to a fabric is *batik.* Other resist materials include clay slip, gum paste, rice paste, resin, starch, or mud. All solidify and prevent dye penetration when the fabric is immersion dyed (Fig. 7). These materials are applied by a variety of hand tools including a brush, pen or *kalam,* wood block, metal block, or stencil. Following the dyeing process the substance is removed by a variety of methods including immersion in boiling water or cold water, ironing, or brushing.

The term *batik* is used by craftsmen today in a more generalized sense than is appropriate for a discussion of Indian textiles, since a variety of resist materials are employed, and batik is very closely associated with the Indonesian wax resist textiles. The term *batik* will not be used therefore, in this catalogue. Instead, the substance used to resist the fabric will be specified when it is known. Craftsmen in Andhra Pradesh, Gujarat, and Rajasthan apply a variety of resist materials in their textile production.

Printing

Hand Block Printing. This type of printing involves direct application of a colorant to a fabric using a hand carved wood printing block (Fig. 8).

Mordant Printing and Dyeing. Mordants are applied to a fabric with a wood block prior to dyeing. The mordant acts as a catalyst between cloth and dye to promote dye penetration. Mordants used in India include alum, soluble iron salts, and tannin.

Tinsel Printing. In tinsel printing a thick substance such as gum is applied to the textile with a metal stencil (Fig. 9). While the gum is still wet, mica is dusted over the textile, but will adhere only to the stenciled areas. In other textiles gold or silver foil is pressed onto the cloth adhering to the gummed areas only, as shown in Figure 1.

Andhra Pradesh, Rajasthan, and Gujarat produce textiles in which a variety of printing techniques are used. Mordant printing and dyeing is seen in textiles of Andhra Pradesh and Rajasthan. In Gujarat and Rajasthan, hand block printing of direct dyes as well as mordant printing and dyeing and stencil printing are practiced.

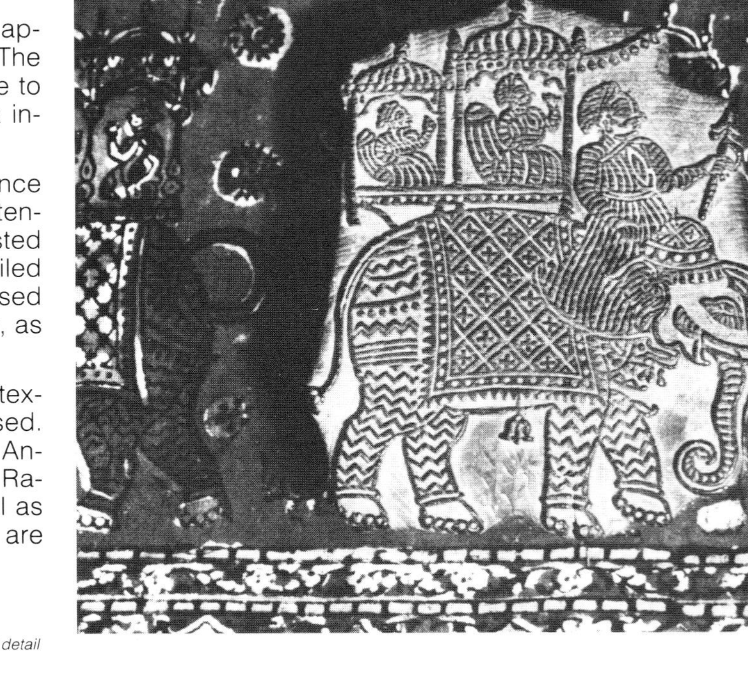

Fig. 8. (Above) Printing block and mordant printed detail from **kalamkari rumal,** *Andhra Pradesh, 58.1-554.*

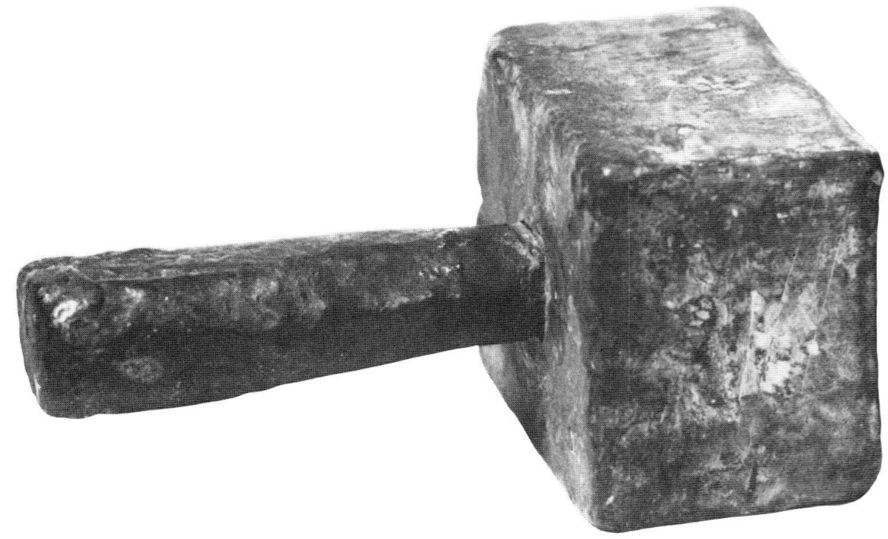

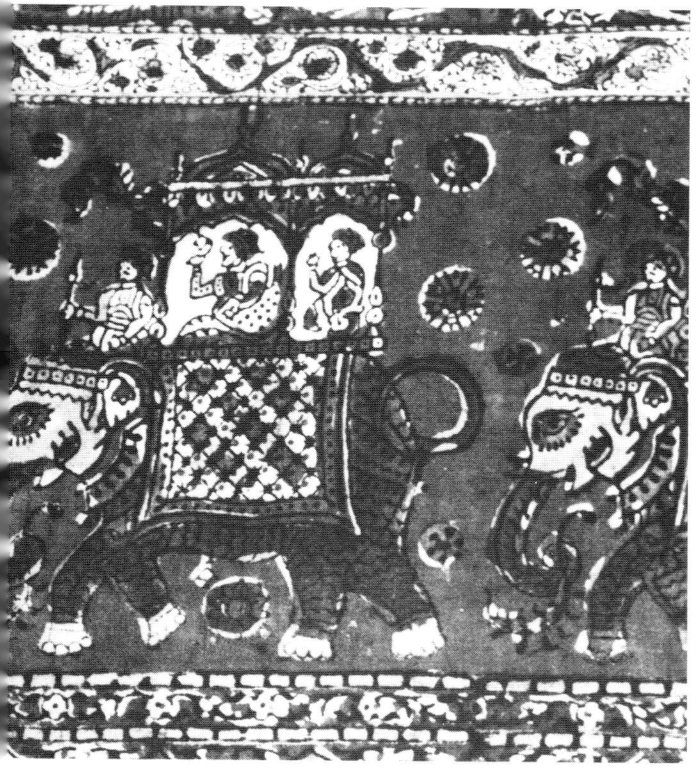

Painting

Dyes, mordants, and pigments may be painted or brushed onto a textile. Dyes and mordants react with the fibers, while pigments lie on the surface of the fabric as in a painting. Painting is practiced throughout Andhra Pradesh, Rajasthan, and Gujarat. The Rajasthani temple cloths of Nathadwara are painted with pigments instead of dyes or mordants.

Combined Techniques

The techniques of printing, painting, and resist dyeing are combined at times in a single textile. One such combination is *kalamkari,* a technique unique to Andhra Pradesh which combines printing, painting, and resist dyeing on cotton cloth. *Ajarak* textiles, made in Rajasthan and Gujarat as well as in Pakistan, use resist dyeing and indigo dyeing in addition to mordant printing and dyeing. In both *kalamkari* and *ajarak* the technique has also become known as the name of the textile.

These selected techniques, illustrated in the textiles of Orissa, Andhra Pradesh, Rajasthan, and Gujarat, are used to produce textiles which are a significant part of the cultural and material heritage of India.

Fig. 9. Wooden mallet and brass stencil box for tinsel printing, Baroda, Gujarat, 58.1-572, p1 & p2.

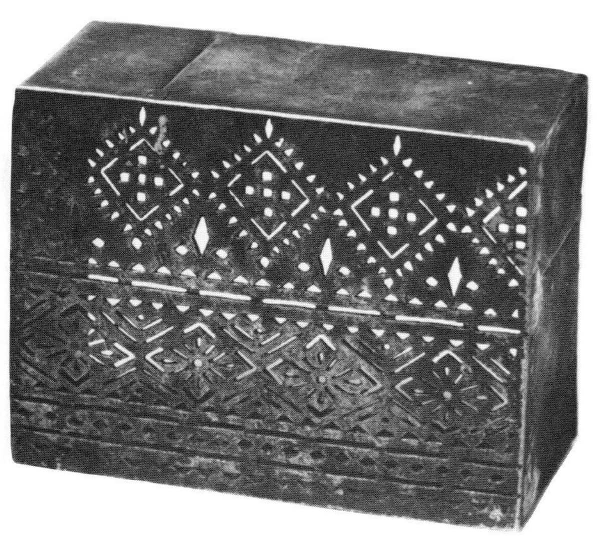

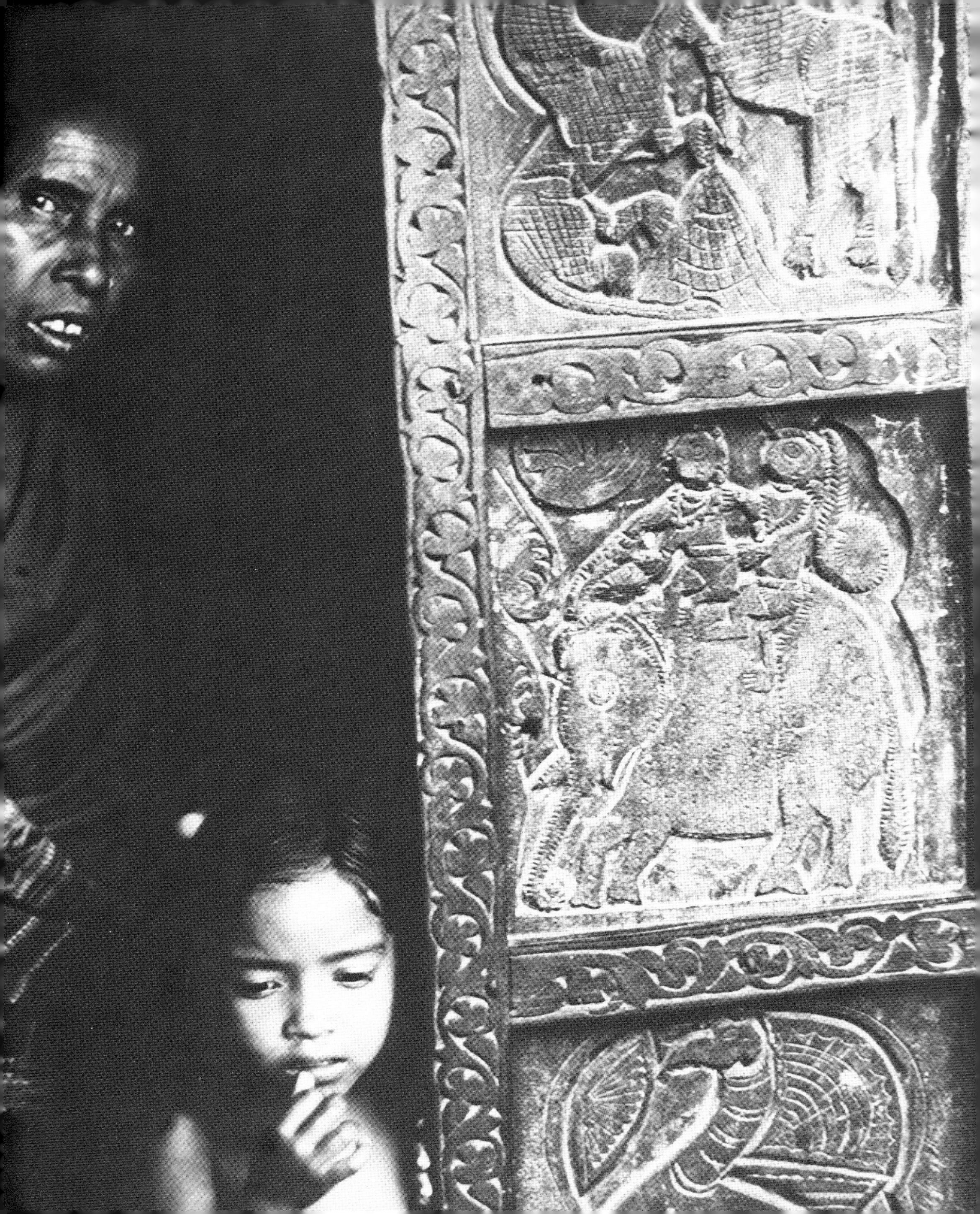

ORISSA

Orissa, a state to the southwest of Bengal, extends along the Bay of Bengal. Its coastal lowlands are dominated by fertile fields of rice which extend into the deep river valleys of the mountainous interior. These mountains have isolated Orissa from neighboring territories. In other parts of India, Orissa has been viewed as a rather remote and backward region that never advanced beyond its ancient fame as the land of Kalinga. Orissa faded from history until India's medieval times when the coastal town of Puri, site of the temple of Shri Jagannath, became a major pilgrimage center. The cult of Jagannath stimulated and sustained a devotional (*bhakti*) Hinduism through a flowering of the regional Oriya language. Spiritual and material cultures merged as a distinctive regional identity evolved in the basin of the Mahanadi River.

There are two areas of ikat production in Orissa: Sambalpur district in the interior and Cuttack district on the coast. In British times Sambalpur was cut off administratively from the rest of Orissa; in addition, the geography of the region contributed to preserving the integrity of a distinctive ikat style. Cuttack, on the other hand, is closer to and therefore influenced by Puri, the political and religious hub of Orissa. The weavers in one Cuttack village, Nuapatna, continue to provide a religious ikat textile for use at the Jagannath temple as well as ikat textiles readily distributed throughout Orissa.

Ikat of Sambalpur District

In the upper Mahanadi River valley of Sambalpur district, village houses stand side-by-side in unbroken lines creating a common linear exterior when viewed from the street. The plain ochre-colored mud wall and high mud *varanda* (veranda) are in sharp contrast to the household doorways, which are richly embellished with carvings. Each doorway is separated into six panels containing carved animal motifs enclosed by continuing floral scrollwork (Fig. 10). Doorways are carved with animal themes that also appear in textiles; elephants and peacocks are, as in textiles, contained within floral borders. This main entrance leads back into an open central courtyard where the activity of the household takes place. Rooms for working, sleeping, and cooking all radiate off this central courtyard. Occupying a prominent position in the plan of the house is the workshop for weaving, which houses the pit loom. Weaving is a fulltime occupation throughout the year except during the summer monsoon season when families usually engage in agriculture or day labor.

Fig. 10. Carved doorway in Jhilminda village, Sambalpur district, Orissa.

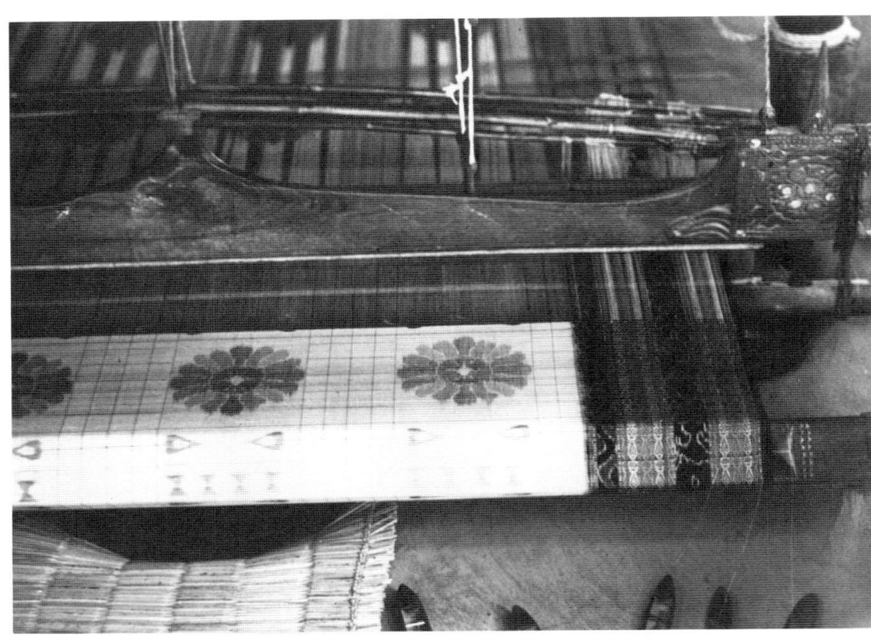

Fig. 11. (Right) Woman of Barpali village, wearing Sambalpur's traditional **domuha** *sari, works on a wooden warping board placed on the ground beside her.*

Fig. 12. Continuing behind the carved reed is the prepared warp ikat with the flower pattern visible. To the right of the breast beam are several polished wooden shuttles used to create the supplementary patterns of the borders.

All preliminary stages leading to the actual work on the loom are performed outside. The first stages—winding off warp threads and tying the ikat resists in both warp and weft threads—include all members of the extended family (Fig. 11). After the warp threads are wound on a warping board, the undyed threads for the ikat resist are stretched onto bamboo frames outside on the veranda. This rectangular frame groups threads for tying while maintaining the proper weaving sequence. Warp threads are folded in quarters or halves when stretched; weft threads are extended on the frame full length. Since a limited number of designs are used, transferring the design to thread is usually done from memory. Small areas of the design are tied with cotton thread, but a dye resistant plant or strips of rubber are used for blocking out larger areas.

After completion of the tying, the men in the community immerse the white cotton threads in dye. Until approximately thirty years ago, vegetable dyes were used exclusively: indigo for blue, and the bark of a local tree, *lodha chhal* (*Symploco racemoze*), for red. Now commercial dyes have replaced them; only a few villages outside Sonepur on the Mahanadi River still prepare vegetable dyes. A distinguishing characteristic of the Sambalpur saris is the limited use of colors. The ground color is either a rich deep red or blue with the ikat dyed in the other color. The *pallu* consists of alternating bands of red and blue. Other colors, including yellow, white, and green, are introduced into supplementary weft and warp patterning in limited amounts. The narrow ikat bands of the *pallu* depict red and blue animals, birds, fish, and flowers outlined in white. Often a vertical white line, which aids registration of the ikat, can be observed on either end of the band. The ikat figures are realistically portrayed, their outlines soft and feathered. As only two threads per knot or binding are tied, the ikat has great clarity, fluidity, and detail.

The loom, a counterbalance treadle loom, rests on the edge of a pit dug into the ground. The male weaver sits on the ground with his legs extended into the pit to work the treadles. The heddle and harness system, rather than being supported by an exterior frame, simply hangs from the ceiling, and the unworked warp is drawn up and hung in back of the loom. The design on the highly polished and carved beater and beam reflects the lotus design in the double ikat pattern being woven in Figure 12.

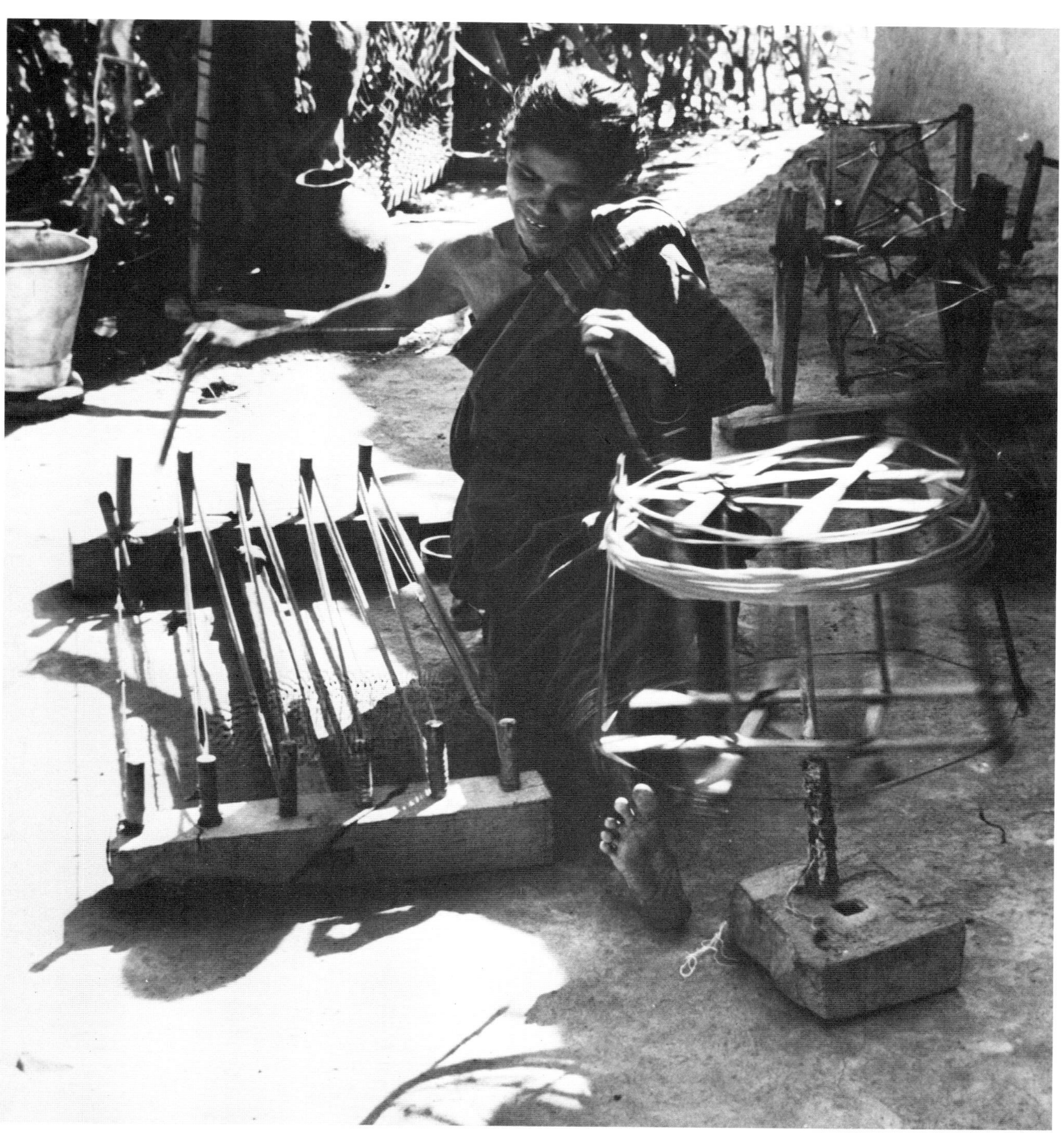

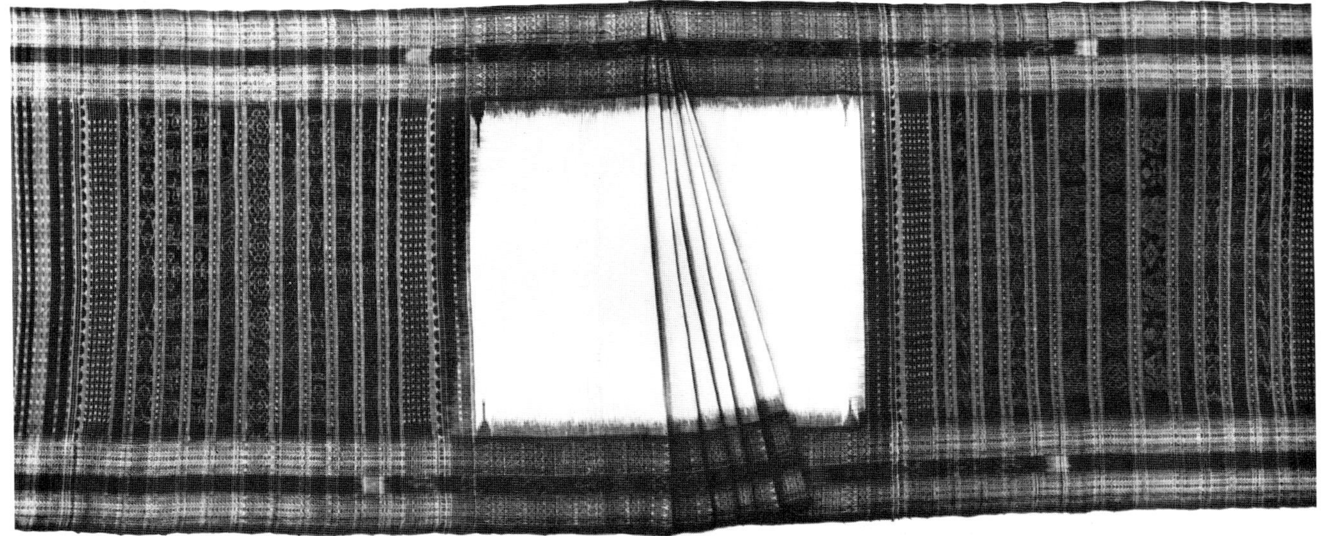

Sambalpur's ikat weaving results primarily in articles of clothing characterized by a distinctive *domuha* ("two faces") sari worn by all the women of this area. *Domuha* indicates an equal width *pallu* at either end of the sari, which frequently has a plain field (Fig. 13). The motifs of the *domuha* sari's ikat *pallu* are also portrayed in the Odissi *pallavi* (pure dance). The *pallavi* dramatizes the ten gaits of the swan, peacock, deer, elephant, horse, lion, serpent, frog, hero, and maiden. People are rarely depicted in Orissan ikat. However, one old Sambalpur sari in the collection at the Weaver's Service Center in Bhubaneswar clearly shows a human form in the center of the ikat band on the *pallu*. Contemporary saris show the same format, but the human form has become an amorphous shape. Another distinctive design element of the Sambalpur sari is *dasphulia*, the ten (*das*) stripes of supplementary warp patterning beginning at each selvedge. The *dasphulia* ("ten flowered") frame and enclose the central field of these saris.

The Sambalpur sari is short, measuring only four yards in length, because of the unique style of wrapping in this area. One *pallu* appears in back from the waist to knees, and the other is draped across the breasts. A *choli* (short blouse) is not worn in Sambalpur.

The plain field *domuha* saris are for everyday wear. The *saktapar domuha* sari and the *bichitrapar domuha* sari with patterned fields indicate their use for special events such as marriages or festivals. The central field of these saris is striped with warp ikat in a wave pattern which encloses either double ikat or woven plaid patterning. In the center of the field is a wide stripe of warp ikat figures.

The *saktapar domuha* sari exemplifies the finest in the Sambalpur style where warp ikat, weft ikat, and double ikat combine with supplementary warp and weft patterning to produce a visually and texturally rich textile. *Saktapar* is the regional name in Orissa for the *chauper* gameboard motif, depicted by double ikat in the central field of this sari (Fig. 14). *Chauper,* a game played throughout India, is a recurrent design element not only in textiles but also in painting and architecture. *Chauper* is played during the marriage ceremony and at the *Kumar Purnima* festival in Orissa.

The *bichitrapar domuha* sari maintains the double *pallu* and the *dasphulia* of both the *saktapar* and the plain field saris, as well as the central warp ikat stripes of the *saktapar* sari. The central field, however, is a woven plaid pattern rather than the double ikat *chauper*.

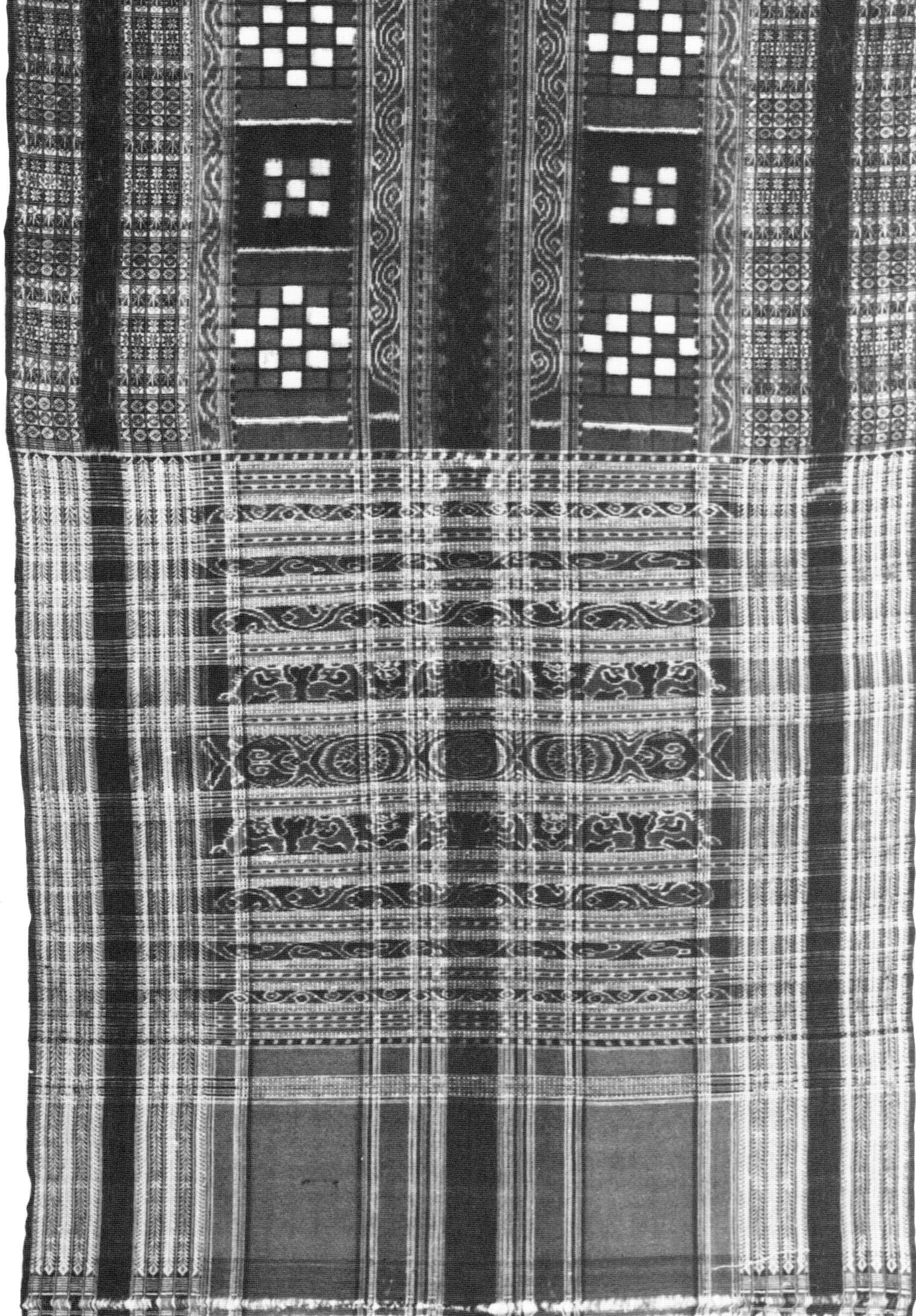

Fig. 13. (Left) **Domuha** sari, Sambalpur district, 20th century (1956). The two **kumbhas** (temple designs) are the only pattern on the plain field and mark the beginning of the pallus. Cotton; warp and weft ikat; warp pattern weave; supplementary weft patterning; discontinuous weft patterning; 4 yd. ½ in. (3.67m) × 1 yd. 1¼ in. (.95m); 58.1-401.

Fig. 14. Detail of **saktapar domuha** sari, Sambalpur district, 20th century (1956). The repeat in the **chauper (saktapar)** designs occurs at the center of the sari indicating a single fold in the warp ikat during tying. Cotton; woven; resist dyed, warp ikat, weft ikat, and double ikat; supplementary weft patterning; warp pattern weave; 4 yd. 3½ in. (3.75m) × 1 yd. 2¾ in. (.985m); 58.1-399.

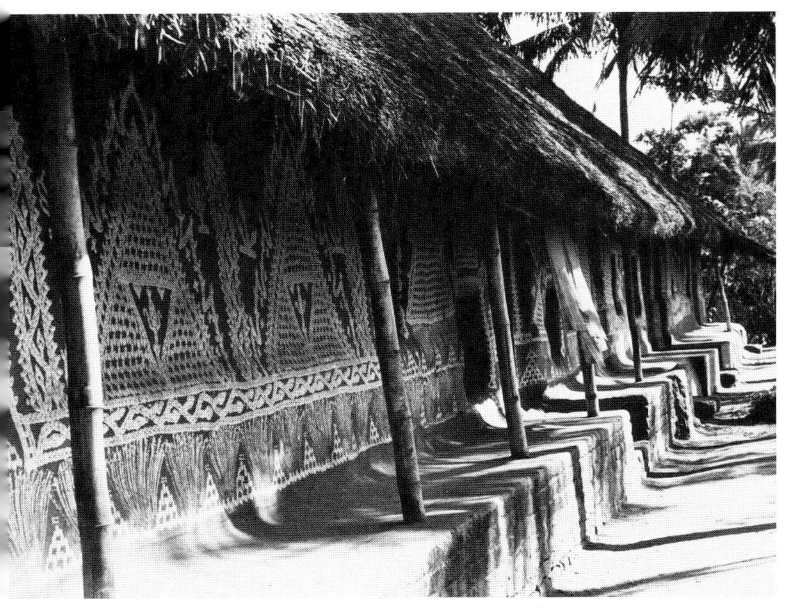

Ikat of Cuttack District

In both Cuttack and Puri districts, the mud-plastered walls are richly and densely embellished with designs, each highlighting a different architectural or structural detail but combining to form an integrated visual statement (Fig. 15). This same system is applied to textiles. Saris are organized into a main field, borders, and a *pallu*. The full length of cloth which meets the ground is defined by a continuous decorative border, while the opposite border becomes a strong diagonal element when draped. The sari's *pallu* is another layer of decoration and when draped, becomes a distinctive contained unit. The sari's individual components are separate design units which combine to produce a unified, overall design. In the sari in Figure 16, the *kumbha* (temple) motif in the field is integrated with depictions of parrots, meandering vines, and lotus blossoms from the surrounding countryside. A floral border provides a base for the *kumbha* corresponding to the temple motif in this wall painting.

The annual occasion of preparing these wall paintings is on the eve of *Lakshmi Puja*. Lakshmi, the goddess of wealth and prosperity, is symbolically invited into the homes, and the women, who prepare the paintings from rice powder and lime mixed with water, compete to attract the goddess to their homes. Included in the paintings are *pad* (small feet), placed at the threshold symbolizing the goddess' entry into the house. The paintings serve a religious purpose and are an annual reaffirmation of the community's beliefs and a reinforcement of traditions. Similarly, the symbols and motifs of the textiles are prescribed by tradition, and individual expression is acceptable within a prescribed framework and format.

The village of Nuapatna, one hundred kilometers west of Cuttack town on the Mahanadi River, is the main area of ikat production in Cuttack district. The main street is wide, with leaf-covered bamboo structures suspended over the street, creating an intimate and usable public space. Weavers use this space for winding off long warps on sticks placed vertically in the ground.

Nuapatna is known for its *tasar* (wild) silk. The *tasar* worms (*Antherala mylitta* and *paphia*) inhabit the humid areas bounded by rivers such as the Mahanadi, Godavari, and Ganges. Villagers gather the cocoons from the *sal* (*Shorea robusta*) hardwood trees in the hills behind Nuapatna three times a year. After the cocoons are harvested, they are boiled in a solution of soda ash for several hours to soften them. Women and young girls reel the silk (only about one tenth of the filament from the *tasar* is reelable) and do the spinning. The filaments from five or six cocoons are reeled together on a bamboo pirn called a *nathva*. This reeled yarn is most often used as warp. Until approximately thirty years ago weavers from this area used only *tasar* and cultivated mulberry silk, but are now using cotton as well.

The ikat designs are tied only two to four threads per binding. Twenty to thirty saris are prepared together, however, the fineness of the threads ensures the clarity of the design. Rather than only relying on the immersion dyeing technique as in Sambalpur, weavers in Nuapatna introduce many more colors by painting them directly on the tied threads while these are stretched on the frames.

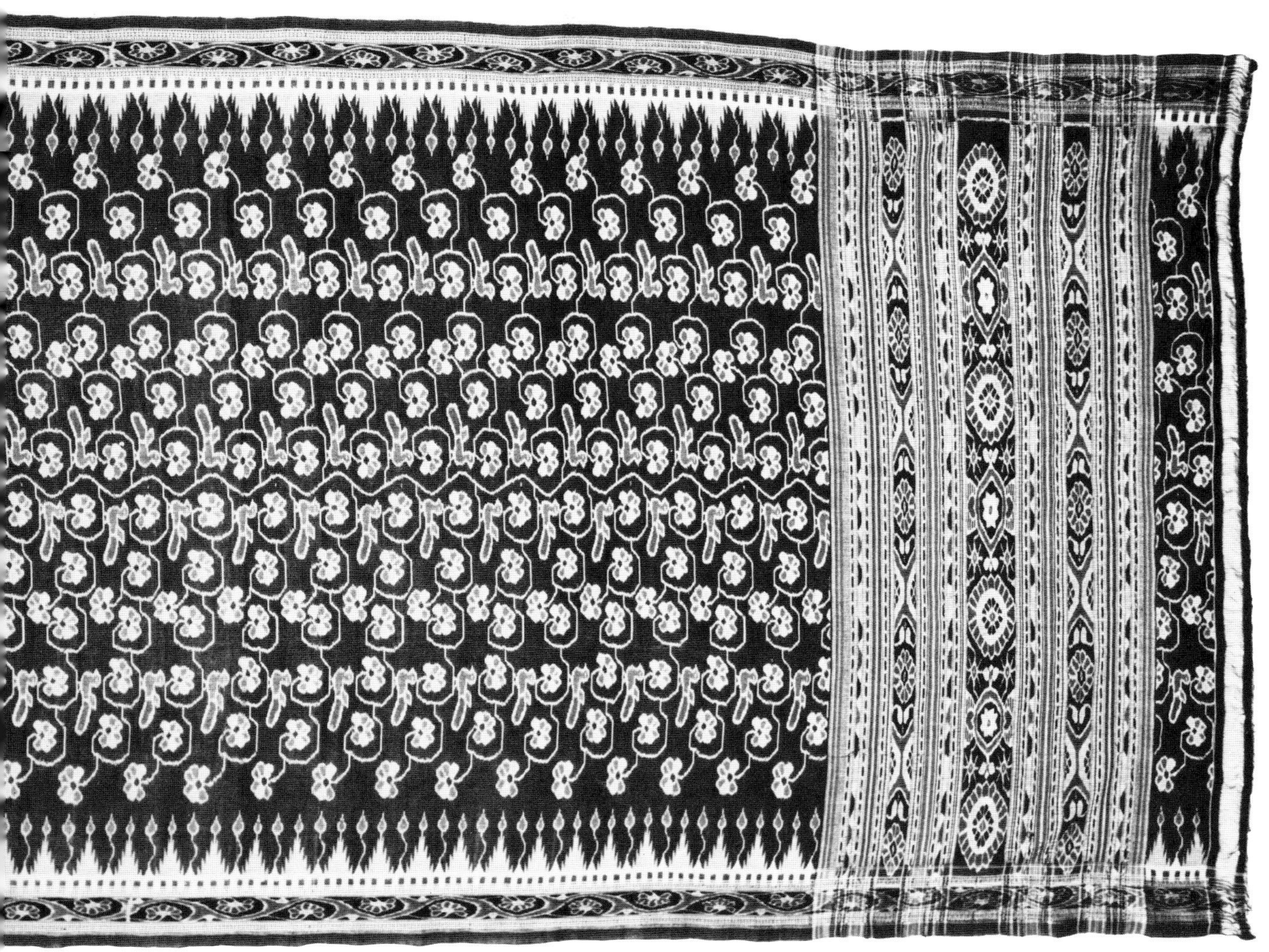

The Nuapatna sari most frequently has a weft ikat field and a single narrow *pallu* consisting of alternating bands of supplementary weft patterning and weft ikat floral motifs. The opposite end is marked by very narrow, solid bands of color. Both traditional and contemporary applications of Nuapatna patterning are reflected in design names such as *muktajhari,* "shower of pearls"; *kumbha,* or temples; *tarabali,* "constellation."

Fig. 15. (Left) The wall paintings on this series of houses in Puri district are prepared annually for the **Lakshmi Puja** *festival, which coincides with the fall rice harvest. The repeated motif on the walls is the* **kumbha**.

Fig. 16. (Above) Detail of sari, Nuapatna village, Cuttack district, 20th century (1956). Cotton helps identify this sari as having been produced in Nuapatna after 1950 when ikat on cotton was first introduced. Cotton; resist dyed, warp and weft ikat; warp pattern weave; supplementary weft patterning; 5 yd. 7¼ in. (4.77m) × 1 yd. 11¾ in. (1.21m); 58.1-387.

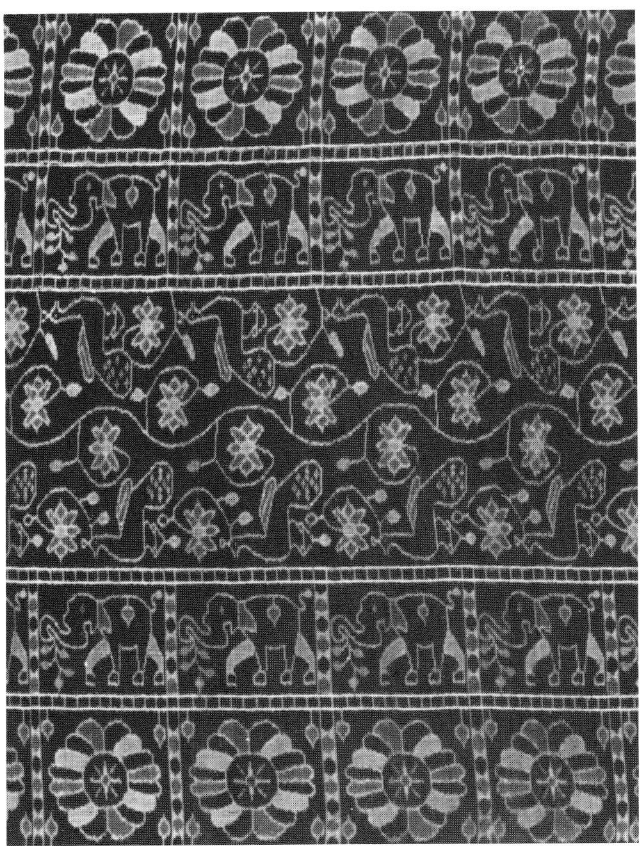

Fig. 17. Detail of **muktajhari khandua** sari, Nuapatna village, Cuttack district, 20th century (1956). The background of this silk sari is black with the ikat figures standing out in white, yellow, and red. Silk; woven; resist dyed, warp and weft ikat; warp pattern weave; supplementary weft patterning; 5 yd. 19¾ in. (5.07m) × 1 yd. 11½ in. (1.21m); 58.1-394.

Fig. 18. (Right) Detail of "**Gitagovinda**" cloth, Nuapatna village, Cuttack district, 20th century. A repeating **shloka** (stanza) from the "**Gitagovinda**" is written in Oriya characters with weft ikat. The **shloka** is indicated by brackets. Silk; woven; resist dyed, weft ikat; 4 yd. 5 in. (3.78m) × 1 yd. 19 in. (1.395m). Courtesy Mr. and Mrs. Jermeja Singh Hundal, Los Angeles.

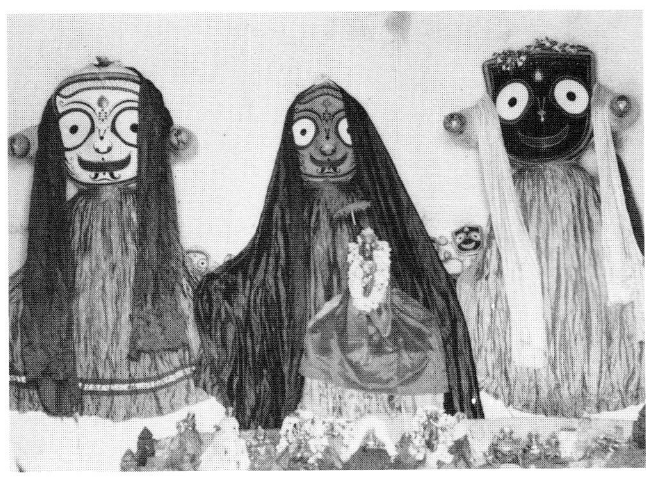

Fig. 19. Jagannath, a manifestation of Krishna, is worshipped throughout Orissa. Silk textiles drape and dress the wooden painted images of Jagannath (extreme right), his brother Balabhadra, and his sister Subhadra in a temple in Gunpur, Koraput district. (Photograph courtesy Eberhard Fischer, Zurich, Switzerland)

The *muktajhari khandua* sari is a weft ikat silk sari with warp ikat borders and contains the traditional format and patterning of another textile, the *khandua*. A *khandua* is an Orissan wedding *odhani* worn over the bride's head during the marriage ceremony. Repeated lotus blossoms and directional elephants are enclosed by rows of pearls. All three elements frame the sari's central panel of meandering vines, lotus blossoms, and peacocks (Fig. 17). The elephant is considered an auspicious animal and is frequently placed on special garments. The *pallu* consists of alternating bands of supplementary weft patterning and weft ikat more stylized than the ikat patterning of the field. The warp ikat borders depict halves of lotus flowers alternately placed along a waving line.

The *"Gitagovinda"* cloth is an extraordinary example of a silk religious textile produced in Nuapatna. It contains a *shloka* or stanza in Oriya characters from the *"Gitagovinda"* executed in weft ikat. This religious devotional poem of the twelfth century by Jayadeva of

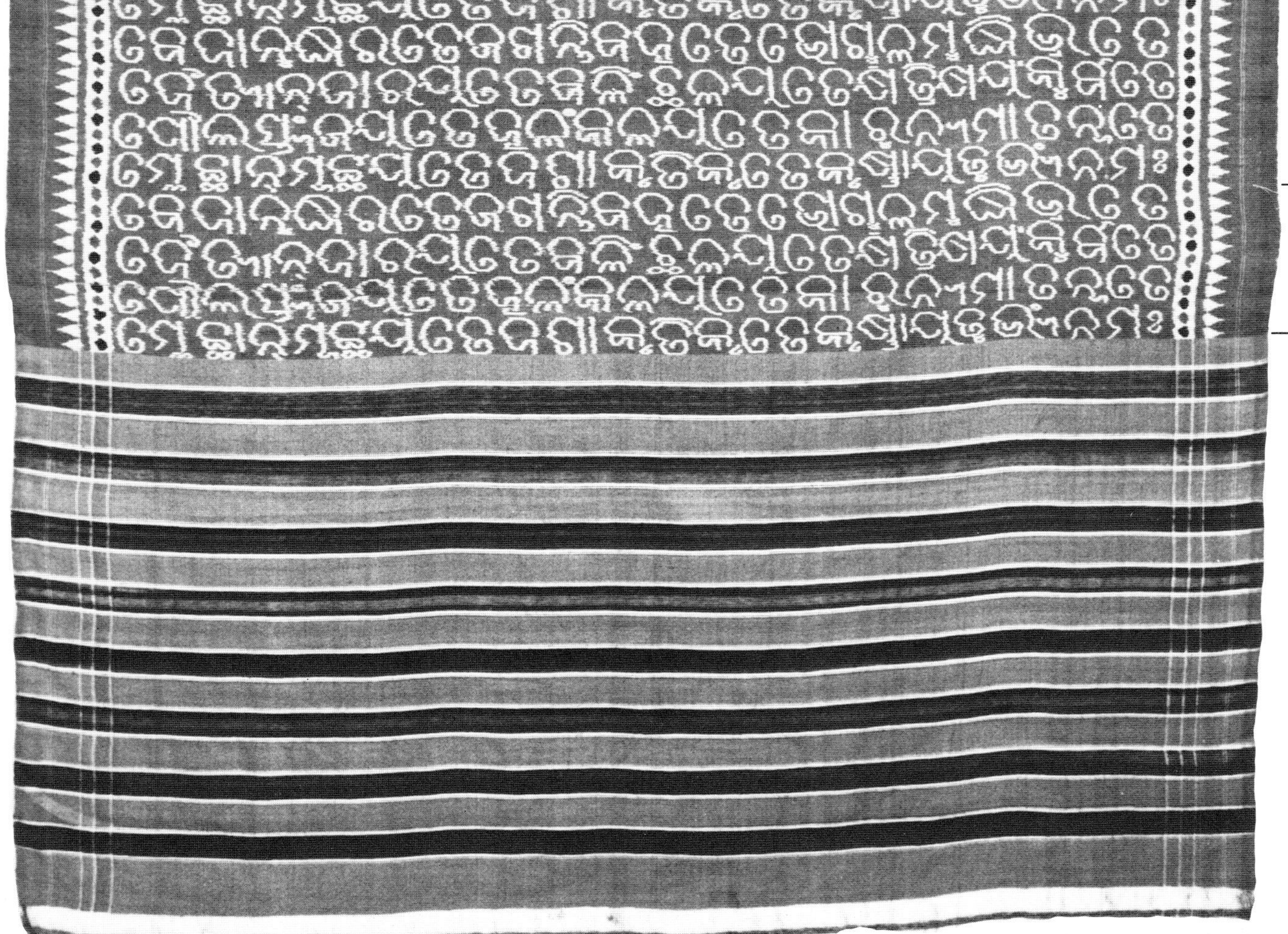

Orissa was written in Sanskrit and is sung daily in the Jagannath temple in Puri. These cloths were also originally produced in Sanskrit, and clerical records from the Jagannath temple with reference to these ikat cloths date back to 1719. More recently the Sanskrit has been transliterated into the Oriya script, as in Figure 18. The *shloka* repeated on this particular cloth is the invocational stanza of the first part of the *"Gitagovinda"* (I:16):

vedān uddharate jaganti vahate bhūgolam udbibhrate
daityān dārayate baliṃ chalayate kṣatrakṣayaṃ kurvate /
paulastyaṃ jayate halaṃ kalayate kāruṇyam ātanvate
mlecchān mūrcchayate daśākṛtikṛte kṛṣṇāya tubhyaṃ namaḥ //

*[Rescuing the Vedas, supporting the worlds, upholding the earth, rending the demons, tricking Bali, destroying the Ksatriyas, conquering Rāvana, bearing the plow, spreading compassion, and crushing the barbarians: I bow to you, O Kṛṣṇa, in all your ten forms.]**

In a community of many weaving families, only one family prepares the *"Gitagovinda"* cloth. The weaver performs a *puja,* a ritually prescribed religious ceremony, before beginning work on the piece and fasts until its completion. The textile covers the sacred log, the *daru,* after its ritual selection from the forest. Only during the year that contains two full moons in the month of *Asadha* (June–July) is a new image of Jagannath selected and carved (Fig. 19). This renewal ceremony, repeated only as prescribed by the lunar calendar, has occurred only five times in the last one hundred years. Jagannath's attending *daitas* (formerly tribals) also wear the *"Gitagovinda"* cloth as a turban or shoulder cloth.

Sambalpur and Cuttack were directly linked to this religious tradition centered in Puri and it seems quite probable that itinerant craftsmen, bringing with them the skills and technology of their area, traveled back and forth along an established pilgrim's route that linked the upper Mahanadi valley with the coast.

*Text and translation by Richard Salomon, Assistant Professor of Sanskrit, Asian Languages and Literature, University of Washington.

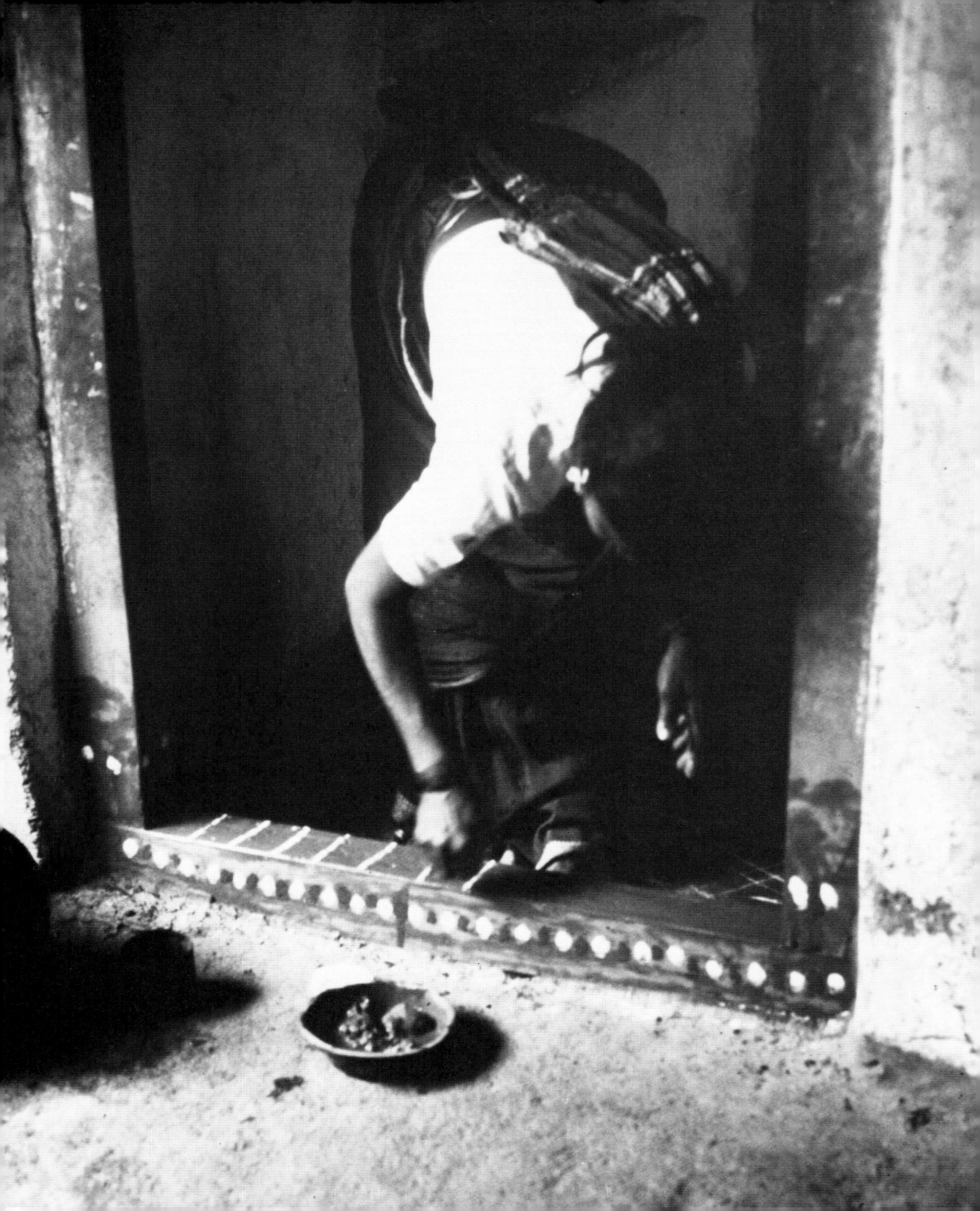

ANDHRA PRADESH

Andhra Pradesh, the state adjacent to and south of Orissa, has a diverse historical heritage. Its primary language is Telugu, one of south India's Dravidian languages. Yet Andhra had a long period of Islamic political domination from the fourteen to the nineteenth centuries. This Muslim presence is still apparent in the survival both of the Urdu language and a substantial Islamic population in and around the city of Hyderabad. During the seventeenth century, Andhra's coast was an important area of contact with Europeans, particularly the Dutch, who sought to exploit the skills of the Andhra craftsmen.

As in Orissa, the craftsmen of Andhra Pradesh use the technique of ikat to produce women's saris as well as a distinctive man's garment known as the *rumal. Rumals* ("handkerchiefs") are small, one yard squares that are usually woven two at a time. Ikat saris and *rumals* are woven in Pochampalli and the surrounding villages. The *telia rumal,* indigenous to Chirala only, refers to ikat *rumals* that have an oily surface. In addition to the ikat technique, a technique unique to Andhra is *kalamkari* ("penwork") which combines printing, painting, and resist dyeing. Clothing, household textiles, and religious textiles are produced by the *kalamkari* technique in the Machilipatnam area and Kalahasti village.

Ikat of Pochampalli and Chirala Villages

Approximately twenty kilometers northeast of Andhra's capital city, Hyderabad, is a group of small villages where ikat textiles are produced. The village of Pochampalli best represents the range of ikat textiles found in this region. In response to climatic conditions, village houses traditionally have high ceilings and peaked roofs made of palm fronds extending down over the veranda. An inner courtyard or atrium is often used for the loom and preparation of the warp.

Pochampalli, devastated by a cyclone and rebuilt in the last twenty years, presents a modern exterior yet the traditional methods of decorating homes have been retained. The women apply fresh red earth and rice decoration to the doorway of the courtyard and around the loom using simple geometric and linear designs to outline the workspace (Fig. 20). Finally, they apply decoration on the outside of the house, graphically defining the work area. This morning ritual, or *puja,* is performed daily before work begins.

Fig. 20. The directness and simplicity of the wall designs parallel the expression of designs in the ikat weaving of this village.

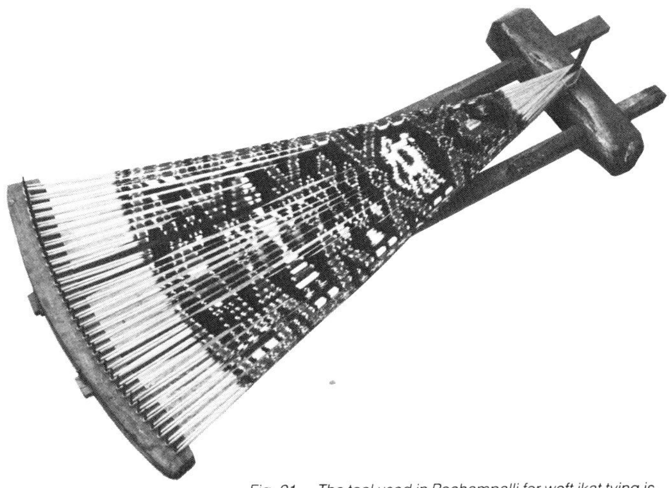

Fig. 21. The tool used in Pochampalli for weft ikat tying is a semicircular frame indigenous to this area. The placement and rendering of elephants and dancing girls seen in this design are strongly influenced by the double ikats of Gujarat (see Fig. 53).

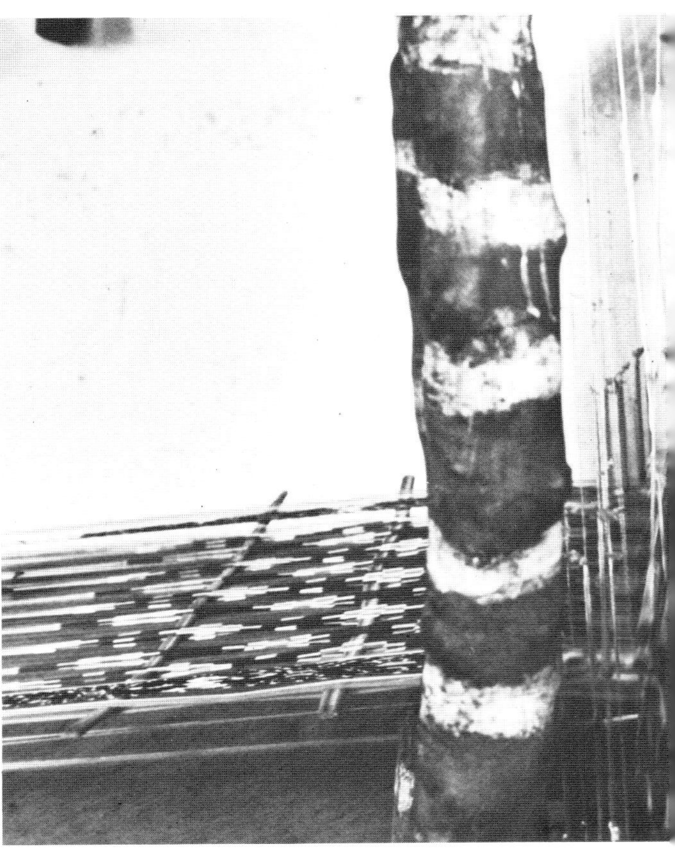

As in Orissa, the courtyard and veranda are used for the preparation of warp and weft. In Pochampalli, threads to be resisted are tied together in groups large enough to produce a stepped geometric pattern. When possible, the warp resists are tied while the warp is stretched full length. The weft resists are tied on a semicircular frame indigenous to and used only in this area. The threads radiate out from a central peg. The crossbar of the frame is adjustable for different widths of weft (Fig. 21).

The Pochampalli weavers belong to the Padmasali subcaste. They claim to be the descendants of Bhrigu Rishi down through many generations of sons to Bhavana Rishi who had one hundred and one sons. These

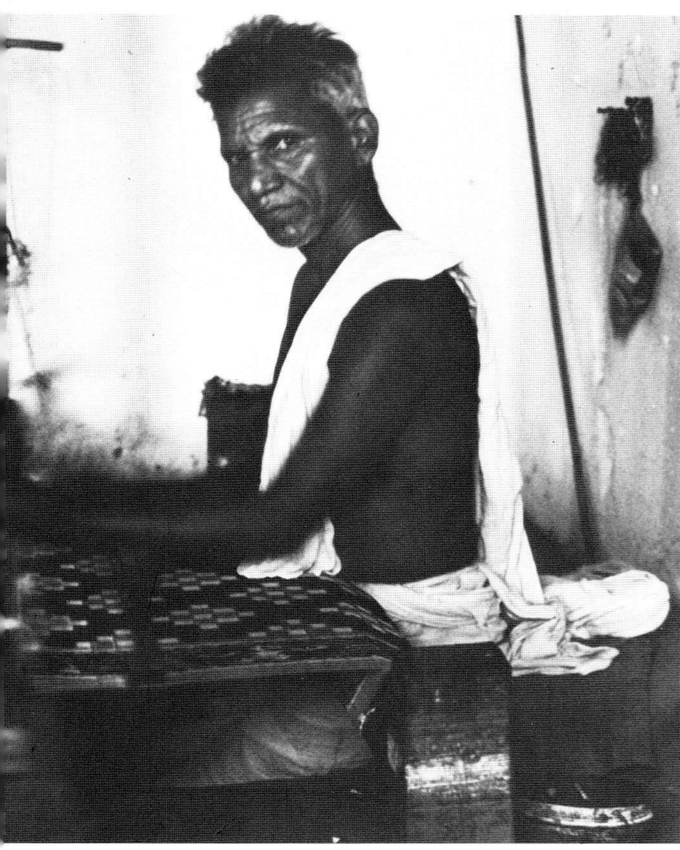

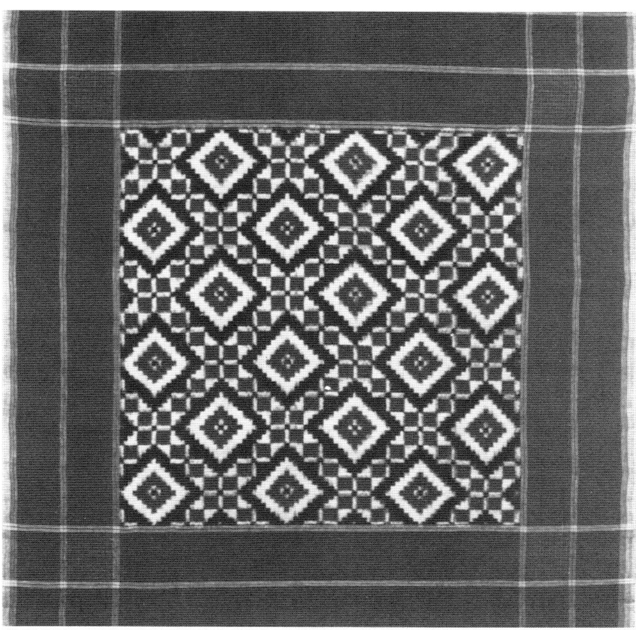

Fig. 22. (Center) The daily ritual decoration of the house extends to the work area and decoration of the pit loom in Pochampalli.

Fig. 23. (Above) **Telia rumal,** *Pochampalli village, Nalgonda district, 20th century. Cotton; woven; resist dyed, warp and double ikat; supplementary weft patterning; 1 yd. 9½ in. (1.16m) × 1 yd. 7 in. (1.09m); 58.1-417.*

sons chose to weave, and the first cloths they wove were out of the fibers of the *padma* (lotus) stem. They therefore became known as Padmasalis. As in most of India, weaving is reserved for the men in the villages, but men and women participate in all other related processes. A distinctive feature of the Padmasali loom is that the beater and harness are supported by a rudimentary frame of two rough posts imbedded in the ground on either side of the pit (Fig. 22).

Until twenty years ago the weavers of Pochampalli were producing double ikat *rumals*. These cotton textiles were characterized by wide, deep red borders that framed the field of double ikat geometric patterning. The arrangement often used a diagonal or square grid system or combined both, as shown in Figure 23. Single *rumals,* one yard square, are worn by men as turbans and wrapped lower garments. Double *rumals* are also worn by men. Pochampalli weavers also formerly made a sari approximately nine yards long known as *janani.* This sari had a plain field and ikat *pallu.* Current ikat production includes a five-and-one-half-yard sari in which the influence of the *rumal's* geometric pattern is evident in the central field. Pochampalli weavers are now also weaving saris that show the influence of Gujarati *patola* and Orissan designs.

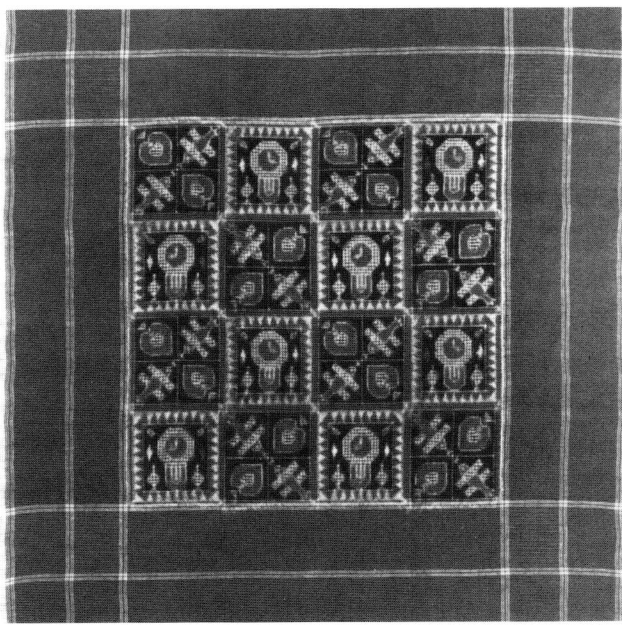

Fig. 24. ***Telia rumal**, Chirala village, Guntur district, 20th century. Cotton; woven; resist dyed, double ikat; supplementary weft patterning; 1 yd. 12 in. (1.22m) × 1 yd. 6½ in. (1.08m); 77.7-237. Harriet Tidball Collection.*

Traditional ikat *rumals*, however, are still being produced in the village of Chirala, Guntur district, a coastal district in southern Andhra. *Telia rumal,* a commonly used term, describes a preliminary treatment of the resist dyed threads which is no longer being used. The threads were repeatedly soaked in an emulsion of earth and oil, a method which gave the *rumals* their distinctive stiffness and oily smell. The presence of *tel* (oil) is useful now as an aid for identifying this group of older cotton ikat textiles. The term *telia rumal* is still generally applied, however, to all ikat *rumals* of Andhra Pradesh. While Chirala *rumals* are no longer oiled, the remaining parts of the process are still the same. The tie dyed yarns are immersed in alizarin paste and boiled for several hours until the desired reddish brown color is obtained. Another distinguishing characteristic is the slight bleeding of the red into other areas, which is common to alizarin dyeing, softening both the colors and the edges of the motifs. As in Pochampalli, wide borders enclose a central ikat field. In contrast to Pochampalli, figurative motifs are used in the central field of Chirala *rumals*. A limited number of motifs are used, including swastikas (*swasti,* "well-being, prosperity"), flowers, birds, and recently, airplanes and wall clocks (Fig. 24).

Kalamkari of Machilipatnam and Kalahasti

Both the Machilipatnam area and Kalahasti village are recognized as major centers for the production of textiles using the *kalamkari* technique. The name *kalamkari* ("penwork") is derived from the technique of applying mordants or resists to cloth using a *kalam* or pen. *Kalamkari* combines a series of processes including the application of mordants by block or *kalam* and the subsequent immersion dye bath for red, resisting with wax, indigo dyeing, and direct application of color by painting. Current distinguishing features of the Machilipatnam style of *kalamkari* are the application of wax resist prior to indigo vat dyeing and the use of printing blocks to stamp mordant outlines onto cloth. In Kalahasti the designs are drawn on directly with the brush or *kalam.* Both methods are exacting and time consuming, the length of the entire process ranging from several weeks to several months.

Machilipatnam (Masulipatam), a seaport city in northeast Andhra Pradesh, is on one of the mouths of the Krishna River which flows into the Bay of Bengal. The English founded their second trading settlement in India in 1611 at Machilipatnam. The port served as a distribution center for Indian textiles bound for European, Persian, and Indonesian markets. In addition to its importance as a port, Machilipatnam and the surrounding villages in the delta area comprised an important center of cotton painting and printing. Local craftsmen produced textiles to satisfy a diverse export and regional market.

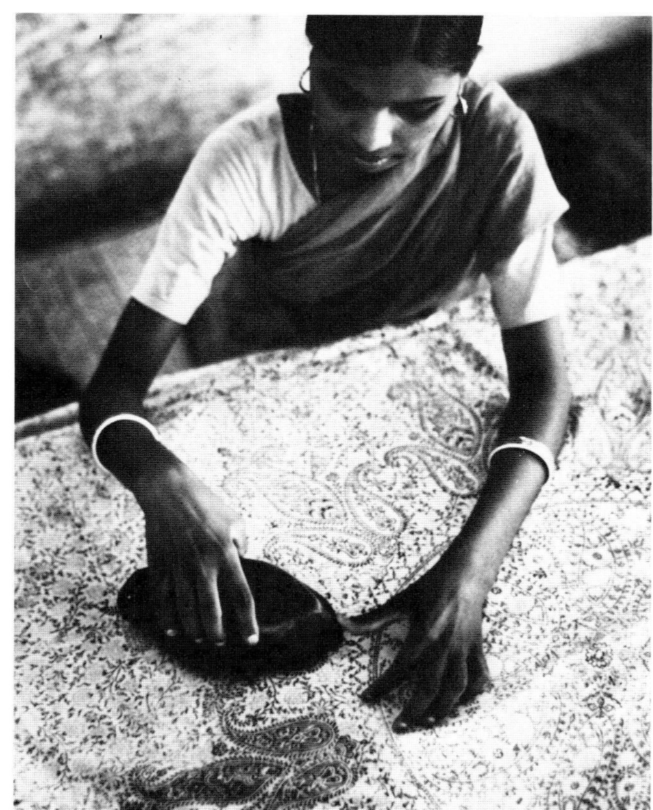

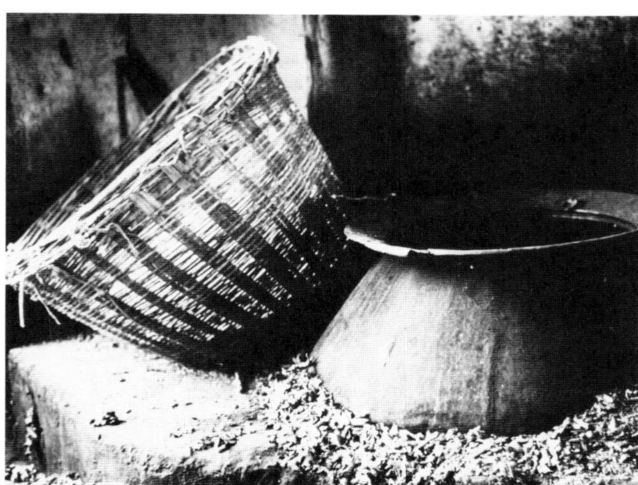

Fig. 25. (Left) A woman, using a wooden block, stamps an alum mordant to cloth carefully registering the block to overprint the mordant onto outlines of the design previously printed with iron acetate.

Fig. 26. (Above) An indigo dye vat and basket of indigo plants in Machilipatnam where indigo is still used in the ***kalamkari*** *process.*

In the Machilipatnam area, printing blocks have been used to outline designs since the nineteenth century. Prior to this time designs were drawn directly with a *kalam.* After a preliminary bleaching, the white cotton fabric is premordanted with tannin. Outlines of designs are then applied with teak wood printing blocks, using an alum mordant solution for red and an iron acetate solution for black outlines (Fig. 25). The cloth is immersion dyed in a red dye bath of *chay* (*Oldenlandia umbellata*) and rinsed. The properties of the Krishna River here along the flood lands and the high proportion of calcium in the sandy, shell-laden soil have been credited for the quality, intensity, and permanency of the colors, especially the reds, obtained from this delta area. Alum is then reapplied, and the cloth is dyed a second or third time for darker shades of red. Violet, if desired, is achieved by adding iron acetate to the alum mordant. White areas are again bleached in a dung solution and starched with boiled rice water to stiffen the cloth and facilitate the application of a wax resist. Beeswax is brushed on with a *kalam* as the resist to reserve areas already colored or to be kept white, and the cloth is dyed in an indigo dye bath (Fig. 26), oxidized for the blue color, and then put into boiling water to remove the wax. After another rinsing, washing, and starching, yellow dye is brushed onto white areas and blue areas to produce green. The textile is then traditionally soaked in an alum solution.

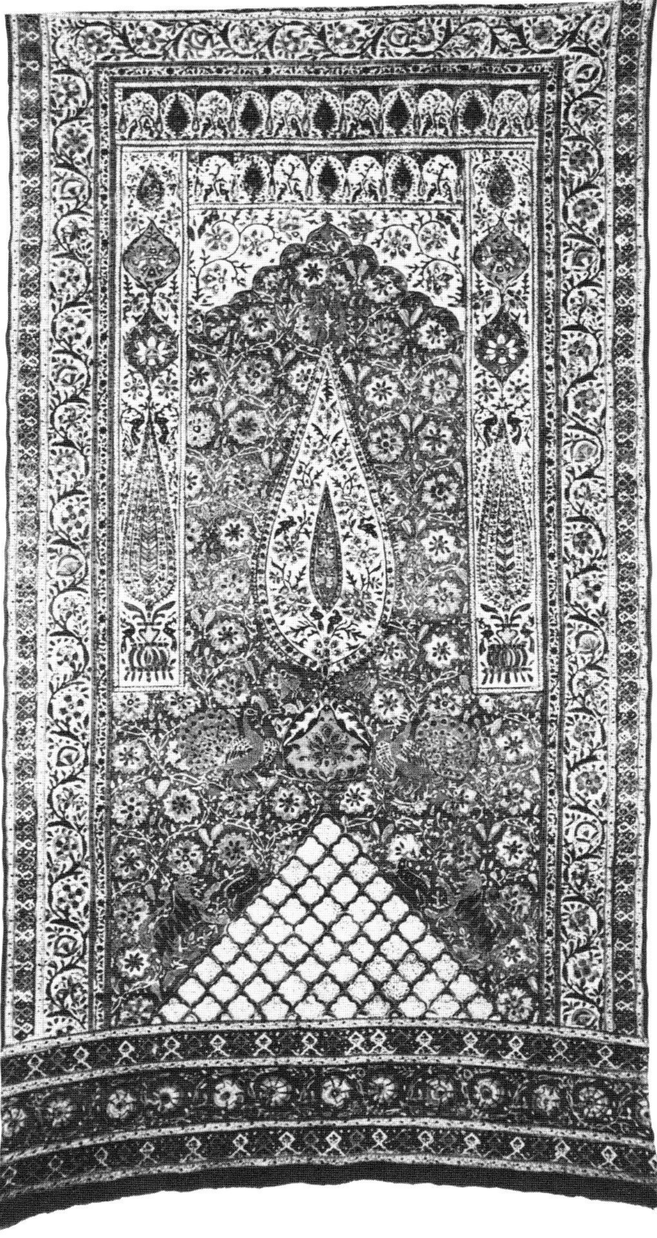

In Figure 27, a *parda* (door curtain) is one of several types of textiles produced in the Machilipatnam style of *kalamkari.* It was made in Balyalagudem, a neighboring village, in 1956. The motif arrangement of a central *mihrab,* or prayer niche, clearly shows the Persian influence. The *mihrab* contains a central cyprus tree filled with intricate floral arrangements. This organic quality is further heightened by the use of tendrils to surround and join the floral patterns. Tigers, deer, and peacocks are also depicted in this densely patterned field.

At Kalahasti in the southern district of Chittoor, *kalamkari* temple cloths are produced for specific purposes within the temple complex. The style of *kalamkari* practiced in Kalahasti maintains the older, more traditional method of outlining features and drawing designs using a *kalam* rather than blocks. The *kalams* used for drawing outlines with mordant solutions are short sticks of bamboo or wood tapering to a point on one end. A reservoir to hold liquid mordant is created by tying a ball of hair, wool, or felt above the point.

The cloth is premordanted by soaking in a solution of powdered *myrobalam* (*Terminalia chebula*) and buffalo milk. *Myrobalam* is a nutlike fruit containing tannin which is dried and ground into a powder. Outlines are often traced lightly with charcoal as a guide for the colorants and mordants which are then drawn on with a *kalam.* Some craftsmen draw outlines directly with the mordants. Black outlines are applied first, using *kasam,* a fermented solution made from *jagri* (brown palm sugar) and iron filings. This solution reacts with the tannin premordant and turns black. Alum is also applied to the cloth with a *kalam* where the background color of deep red is desired. The cloth is then washed in river water, dried in the sun, and dyed in a hot vat of madder root, *surudu* root (sassafras) and

Fig. 27. (Left) ***Kalamkari parda*** *(door curtain), Balyalagudem, Krishna district, 20th century (1956). Cotton; woven; printed, hand blocked; resist dyed with wax; indigo dyed; painted; 2 yd. 25¾ in. (2.48m) × 1 yd. 13 in. (1.25m); 58.1-551.*

Fig. 28. (Right) ***Kalamkari*** *temple cloth, Kalahasti village, Chittoor district, 20th century. Cotton; woven; mordant and direct painted; 3 yd. 2½ in. (2.81m) × 1 yd. 14 in. (1.27m). Courtesy Lowie Museum of Anthropology, University of California at Berkeley. (Photograph courtesy Santa Barbara Museum of Art)*

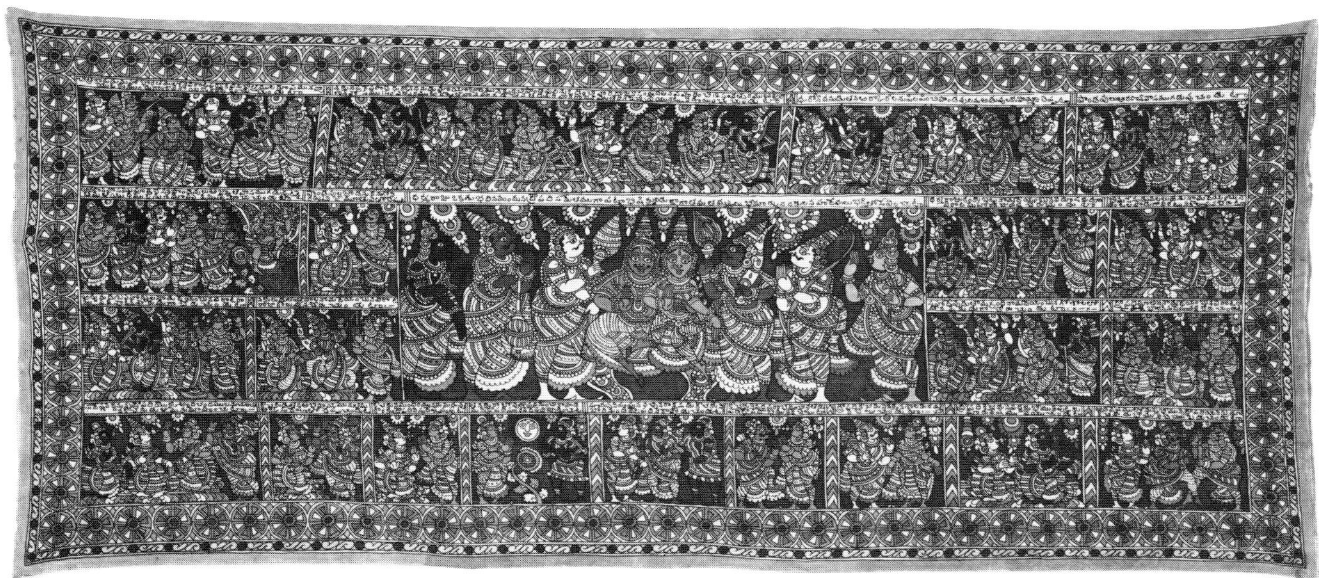

pobbaku (a water reed) to produce deep red. After rinsing in river water to remove the dyes in unmordanted areas, the cloth is bleached by soaking in a solution of sheep dung overnight and dried on the river bank the next day. This process is repeated over a period of a week until the background is pure white. The cloth is then dipped in buffalo milk which prevents the dye colors from spreading when the figures are later painted with yellow and blue. A solution of alum and yellow dye from the dried flowers of *myrobalam* are painted onto the cloth with a *kalam.* Female figures are usually painted yellow. Blue is applied with a *kalam* to depict the *devatas* (gods or divine beings). The *rakshasas* (guardians) are green where blue has been painted over yellow. In the past resisting with wax was used to allow vat dyeing in indigo for blue. It is also possible that indigo in some sort of binder solution may have been directly applied to these cloths. However, today a synthetic blue dye is used.

The subject matter depicted in these *kalamkari* of Kalahasti is strictly religious. They are intended for use in the temple shrine and as decoration for the *rath* (processional cart). The *kalamkari* of Kalahasti most closely reflect the greater Hindu tradition by the pictorial retelling of stories from the *"Ramayana"* and *"Mahabharata"* and function in much the same way as temple murals, paintings, and sculpture. The temple cloths can be quite intricate, many-layered works with the most prominent panels devoted to the main deities or popular themes, such as the marriage of Rama and Sita, as shown in Figure 28. Rows of figures subsequently illustrate other events or important episodes in their lives. In the uppermost band is a scene of men playing a game of *chauper* and in the extreme left is the god Ganesha. Additional information about the episodes is supplied by the small bands of narration in Telugu, the regional language of Andhra Pradesh and in the family of Dravidian languages of southern India.

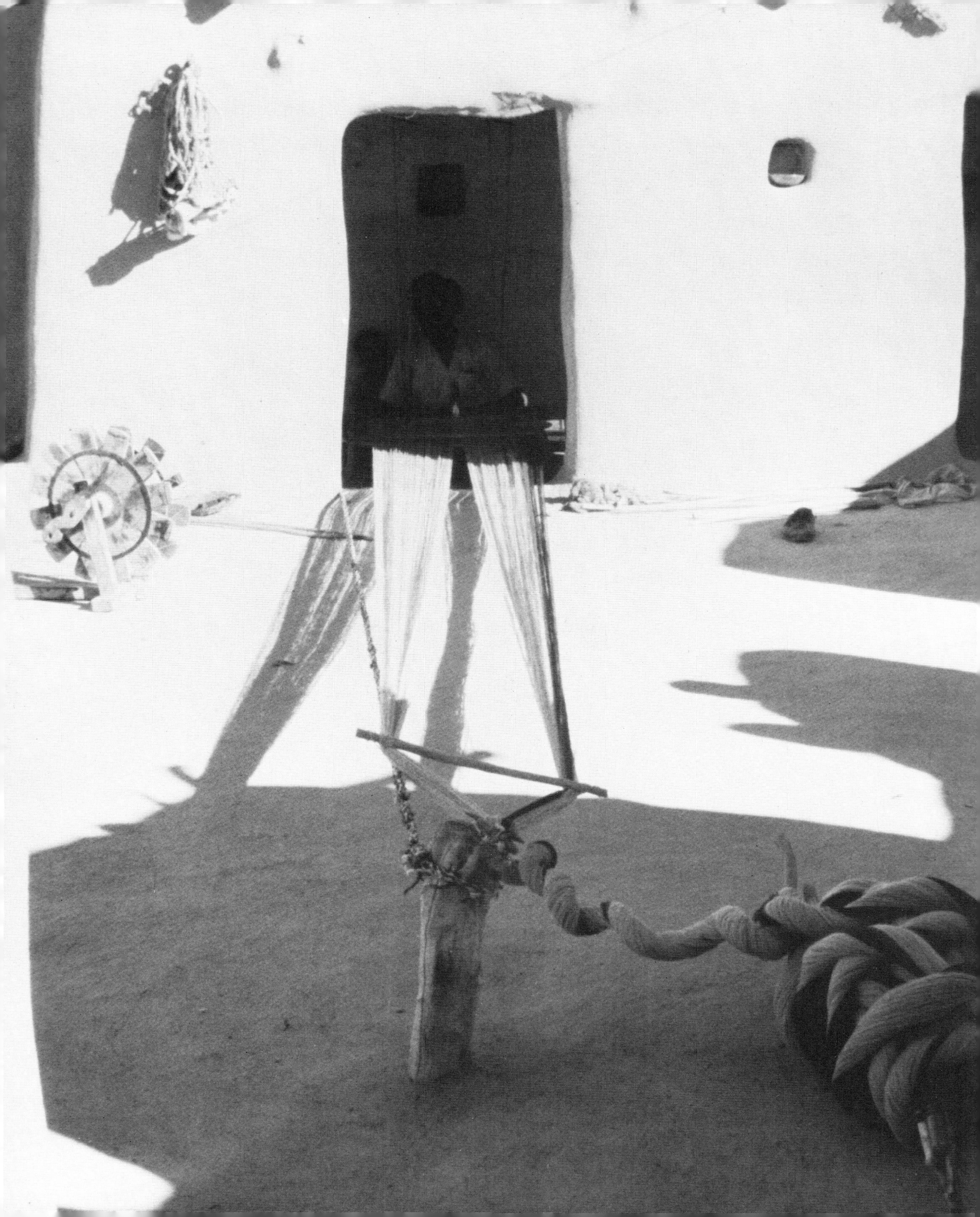

RAJASTHAN

Rajasthan (the abode of kings) is located on the western frontier of today's India. The kings were Rajputs, a self-consciously martial elite whose ancestors had invaded the subcontinent in early times. Their strength of arms held off Muslim conquest for several centuries, and during the time of the Mughal empire the Rajputs were treated more as allies than as conquered peoples. During the British domination, Rajasthan remained mostly under indirect rule in a number of princely states which preserved the courtly life and traditions of Rajput nobility. The region lies between two major river systems of the subcontinent, the Indus and the Ganges, but does not receive much rainfall. Predominantly flat, barren tracts of desert land, the monotony of Rajasthan's landscape is broken by severe outcroppings of ancient rock upon which the Rajputs built their fortresses.

Textile techniques used in Rajasthan include *bandhana*, combinations of resist dyeing, printing, and painting, and direct painting with pigments. The *bandhana* technique includes tie and dye and bound resist. *Ajarak* textiles combine mordant printing, resist dyeing, and indigo dyeing to produce cloths recognizable by their characteristic white, blue, pink, and red patterning.

Bandhana

Outside of Rajasthan's cities are groups of small villages. As in the rest of rural India, the existence of an economic network between the villages in Rajasthan allows for a wider distribution of goods, including textiles. Som, a village located west of the fortress city of Jaisalmer in the Thar Desert, illustrates this exchange. The weavers of Som are the Chamars, traditionally a leather-working caste, and the Bhils, a tribal group. Both weave blankets that are exchanged between Som and with neighboring villages in Rajasthan for *bandhana* turbans and *odhanis*.

Fig. 31. Extending into the courtyard is the wool warp for the ***dhabla****. The courtyard is also used for spinning on the* ***charkha****, a wooden spinning wheel often embossed with brass.*

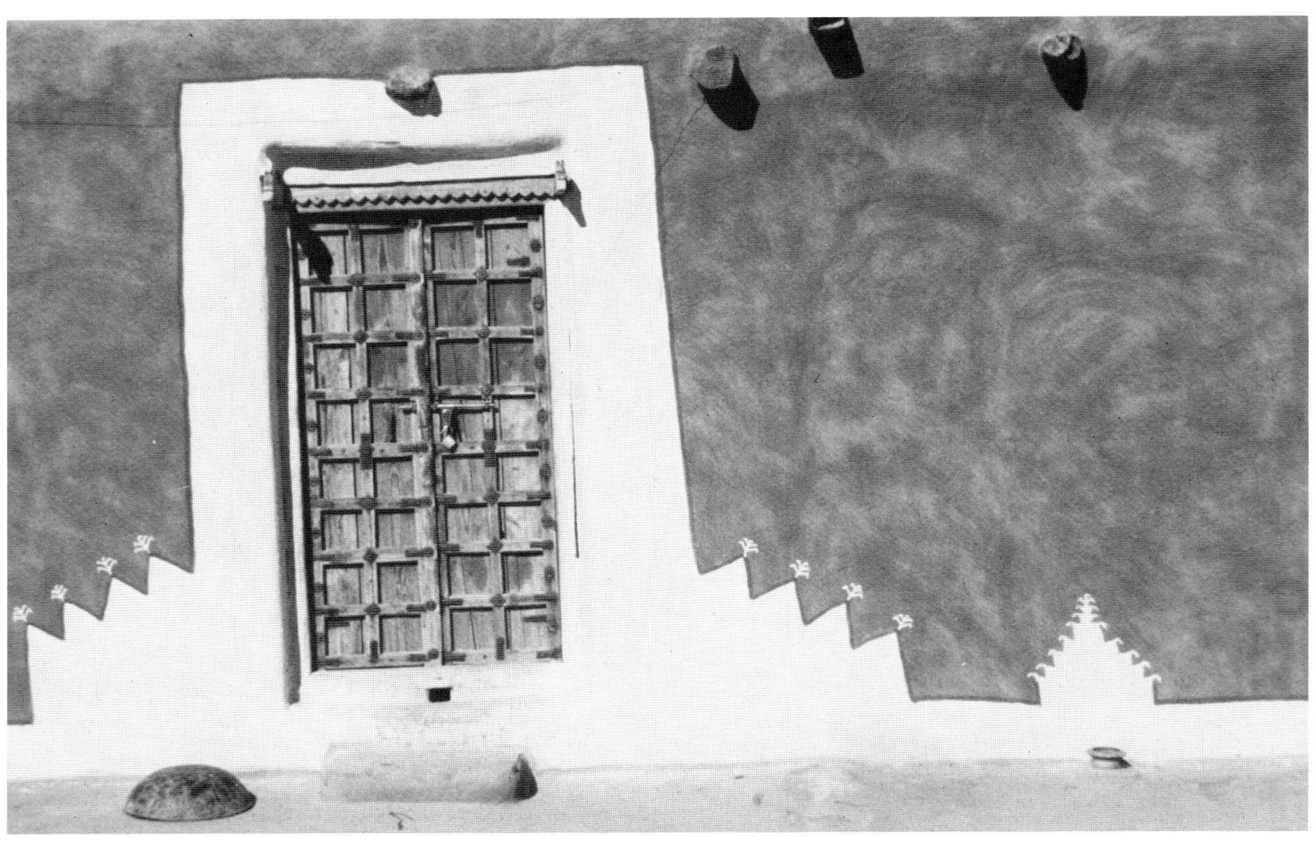

The individual family residence in Som consists of three mud-plastered, flat-roofed buildings which form three sides of the open courtyard. The arrangement of buildings around an open courtyard in Som typifies village architecture in western Rajasthan. The front of the courtyard is an outside wall approximately four feet high. The two facing buildings on the sides of the courtyard house the cooking room and the loom room. The largest building at the back of the courtyard is the sleeping and storage room. The doorways leading to the cooking and sleeping rooms are boldly decorated with white wall paintings (Fig. 29), and the geometric patterning dramatically outlines the wooden doorway. To the right of the doorway, a temple motif is painted; this is a common design motif woven not only into the textiles produced in Som, but also into those from the western rural parts of both Rajasthan and Gujarat (see Fig. 47). The interiors of both the cooking and sleeping rooms are richly decorated with white mud relief work which creates small storage niches and wall designs (Fig. 30). Some of these designs contain mirrors, which are also incorporated into the embroidery of western India. The loom room opens onto the courtyard which allows the weaver to tension his long warp on a post in the courtyard (Fig. 31). The weaver can then be involved with the family's activities in the courtyard as he works.

The most distinctive item of the Rajasthani man's dress is the *pagri* (turban). The *pagri* has been retained, while other traditional garments are being replaced with western-style clothing. Historically, the patterns on *pagris* indicated a season, holiday, or wearer's village. Today the wrapping style continues to convey this sense of regionality (Fig. 32).

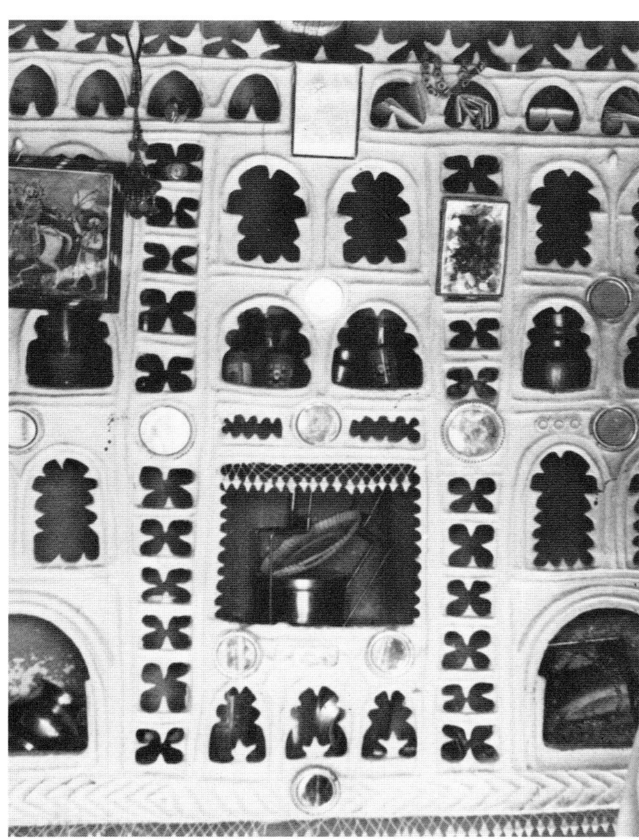

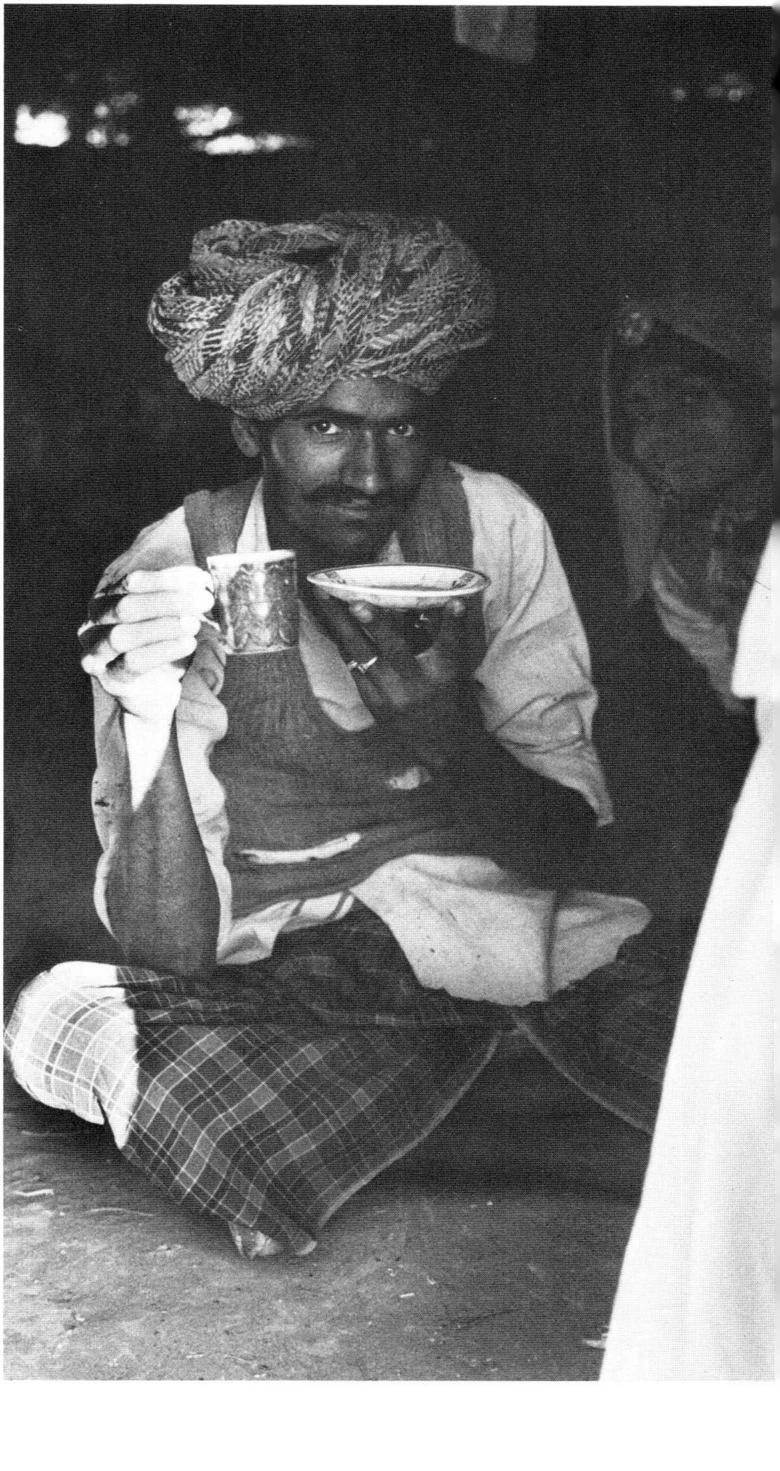

Fig. 29. (Left) The doorway, the most important part of the house, is graphically and dramatically outlined on the Rajasthani desert house of the Chamars in Som village. The building is further defined by the large band that separates it from the ground. The temple motif on the right, by its symbolic placement in the immediate environment of the home, shows the significance of religion.

Fig. 30. (Above) The mud-plastered relief work on the walls provide a visual and textural richness to the interiors of Rajasthani homes.

Fig. 32. (Right) A Bhil man from Som village wearing a **satrangi laheriya** *(seven-colored wave design) turban.*

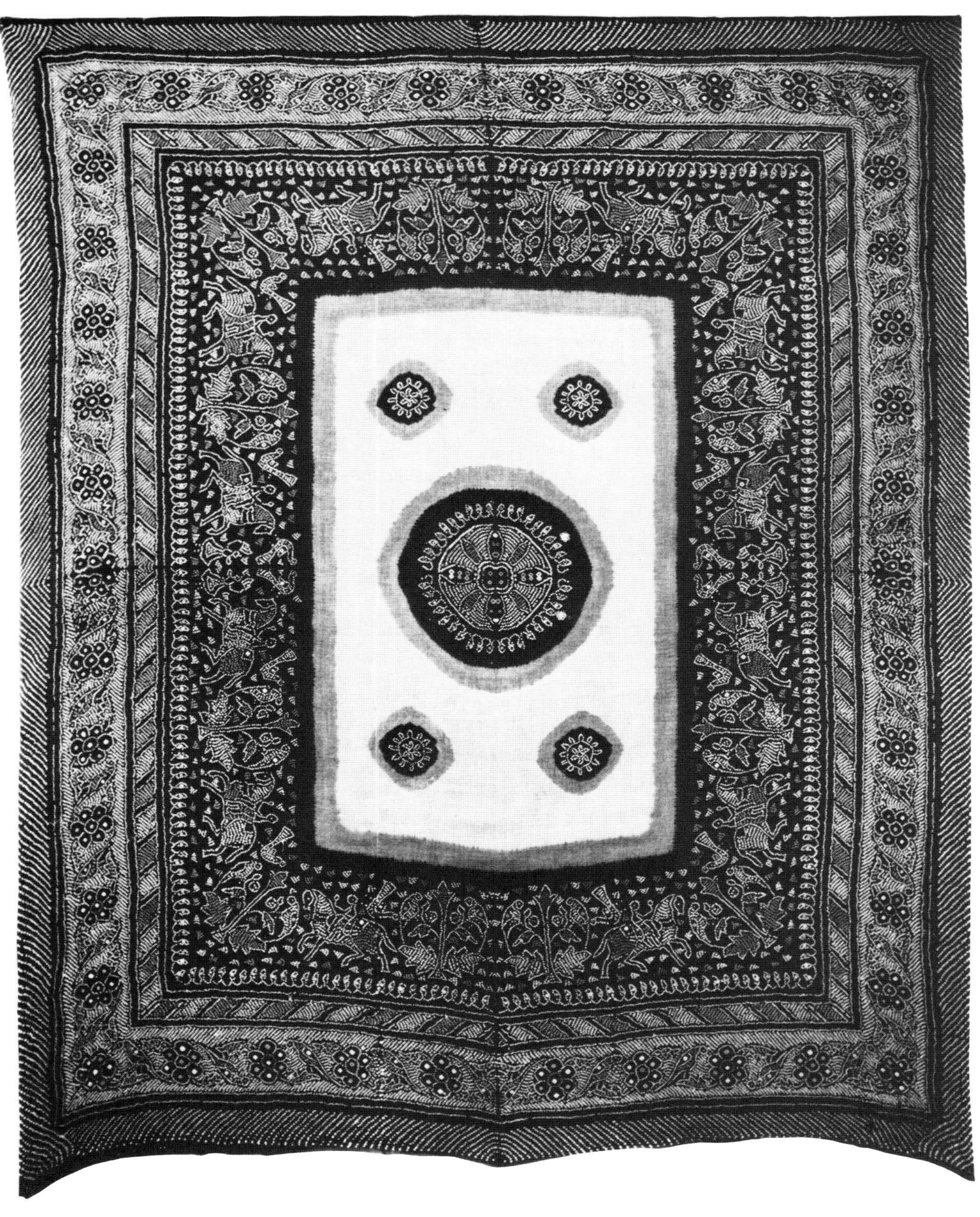

Bound resist turbans are called *laheriya* ("wave design"). The woven cloth is rolled into a coil, and sections to be resisted are tightly bound. The fabric may be rolled diagonally or from end to end producing a striped pattern. A plaid pattern seen on some turbans is produced by retying and dyeing in opposing directions. Turbans may have up to seven colors which are created by repeated resists and dye baths. Historically, the *laheriya pagris* were associated with the Hindu festival of *Teej* and were produced and worn in Jaipur.

Jaipur, a center of *bandhana* production, is a planned city organized on a rectangular grid pattern, designed by Jai Singh II in 1729. The main bazaar lies between the city's two main intersections which are called the *Bardi* (large) *Chauper* and the *Choti* (small) *Chauper*. Wide avenues are flanked on either side by small stalls and stores of the bazaar in which brassware, painted blue pottery, inlaid jewelry, and *bandhana* textiles, including turbans, saris, *odhanis* (headcoverings), and *ghagharas* (skirts) are sold. The *odhani* and *ghaghara* combined with a *choli* are Rajasthani women's traditional clothing. All three are often patterned with *bandhana* resists, printed, or embellished with embroidery. An *odhani* from Rajasthan shown in Figure 33 features a central *bandhana* medallion in a field of yellow framed by several *bandhana* borders. The largest border portrays men on horses, parrots, and peacocks. At the horizontal fold are mirror image women holding fans.

Combined Techniques

Hand block printing is the primary technique for many textiles in Rajasthan which combine resist dyeing, printing, and painting. A few miles west of Jaipur is the town of Sanganer, an important center of hand block printing. While production today does not compare to the high volume of the eighteenth century, Sanganer continues to produce a significant volume of block printed textiles. Until approximately 1940 the Sanganer prints were readily identified by the tariff stamp on the back of the cloth (Fig. 34). The eighteenth- and nineteenth-century fabrics show a remarkable clarity and precision both in execution and in motif detail.

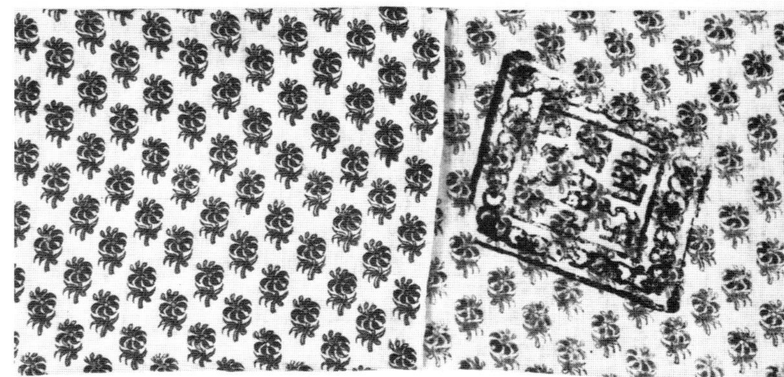

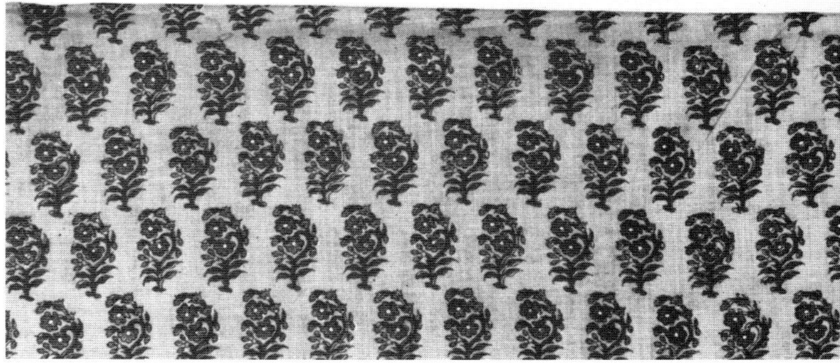

Fig. 33. (Left) ***Bandhana odhani**, Rajasthan, 19th century. This **odhani** was folded in quarters prior to tying which was simultaneously done on all four layers. Cotton; woven; resist dyed, **bandhana**; metal embroidery; 2 yd. 9½ in. (2.07m) × 1 yd. 31½ in. (1.72m); 58.2-52.*

Fig. 34. (Above) Detail of block printed turban fragments, Rajasthan, 19th century. Top: 18½ in. (.47m) × 31½ in. (.80m); 58.2-64; center: 13½ in. (.34m) × 28 in. (.71m); 58.2-62; bottom: 17 in. (.43m) × 27 in. (.68m); 58.2-63.

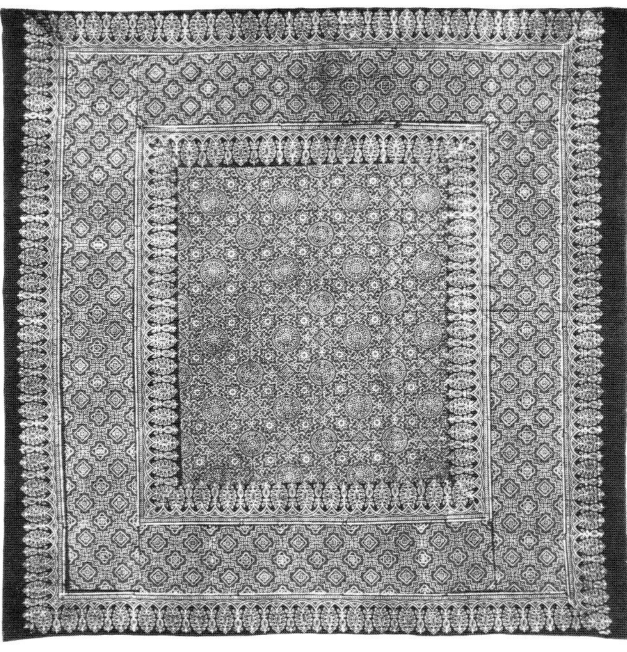

Fig. 35. (Right) *Muslim man wearing an* ***ajarak*** *shoulder cloth in the Jaisalmer cloth bazaar.*

Fig. 36. (Above) ***Ajarak rumal****, Barmer district, 20th century. Cotton; woven; hand blocked with mordant (printed on both sides); resist dyed with clay; indigo dyed; 1 yd. 3¾ in. (1m) × 1 yd. 5 in. (1.04m); 58.1-559.*

The three nineteenth-century turban fragments shown in Figure 34 are decorated with small *butis,* repeated floral designs, that conform to a classic mango or cone shape. The stem and flowers taper in at the top, curve slightly to the left, and are gracefully and naturally portrayed. They were produced by a combination of techniques with slight variations in each piece; however, the processes and dyes used are not directly evident by studying the textile alone. Pattern outlines in the top fragment were mordant printed with alum for red and may have been direct printed with dark green. Outlines of the motif in the center and bottom fragments were printed with a solution of iron salts for black. Gold, the background color in the top and bottom fragments, was probably dyed with *haldi* (turmeric). In both the top and bottom fragments small areas of white appearing in the motifs may have been discharge dyed initially prior to any printing or may have been resisted with an unknown substance to allow later immersion dyeing. Additional accent colors of violet, green, and deep pink may have been direct printed.

Historically, block printed turbans with floral patterns were associated with *Dashera,* a ten-day religious festival commemorating Rama's victory over Ravana. This festival is an important one in Rajasthan, because it celebrates the heroic spirit of Rajasthan's history.

Another group of textiles which combines printing and resist dyeing is the *ajarak* fabric produced in Rajasthan, Gujarat, and the Sind area of present-day Pakistan. The word *ajarak* is derived from the Arabic *azraq* ("blue"). To produce *ajarak,* a complex combination of block printing with mordants, resist dyeing, and dyeing in alizarin and indigo is used. The result is an intricately patterned cloth for men's turbans and shoulder cloths (Fig. 35). The textile is characterized by dominant blues, pinks, and reds with white and occasionally black to add depth and to outline patterns. In Figure 36, three patterned frames enclose the central field of circular medallions surrounded by floral motifs and eight-sided stars. The medallions represent the carved *chakki* (millstones) used in India to grind grain.

Ajarak is another process not immediately evident from direct observation of the textile alone. The printing and resisting process, as detailed in available literature, includes many steps. The cloth is first washed, bleached, conditioned, and softened with various mixtures of *tamarind* seeds, soap, soda ash, and oil. Black outlines are printed with a thick mordant solution of gum, clay, and iron sulfate; white designs with a solution of gum and lime; and pink areas with a mordant solution of gum, alum, clay, and a small amount of alizarin. All of these areas are then resisted with a mixture of clay, flour, and gum. After fixing with a solution of rice water and cow dung, the cloth goes into an indigo dye bath for blue and is then boiled in an alizarin dye bath for the red. After rinsing, a second resist is applied as is a second mordant for dyeing deeper shades of red. After a final rinsing in soda ash, soap, and cow dung, the cloth is beaten and polished to soften it. *Ajarak* textiles are sometimes printed, resisted, and indigo dyed on both the front and back sides, which is possible because a clay resist is used.

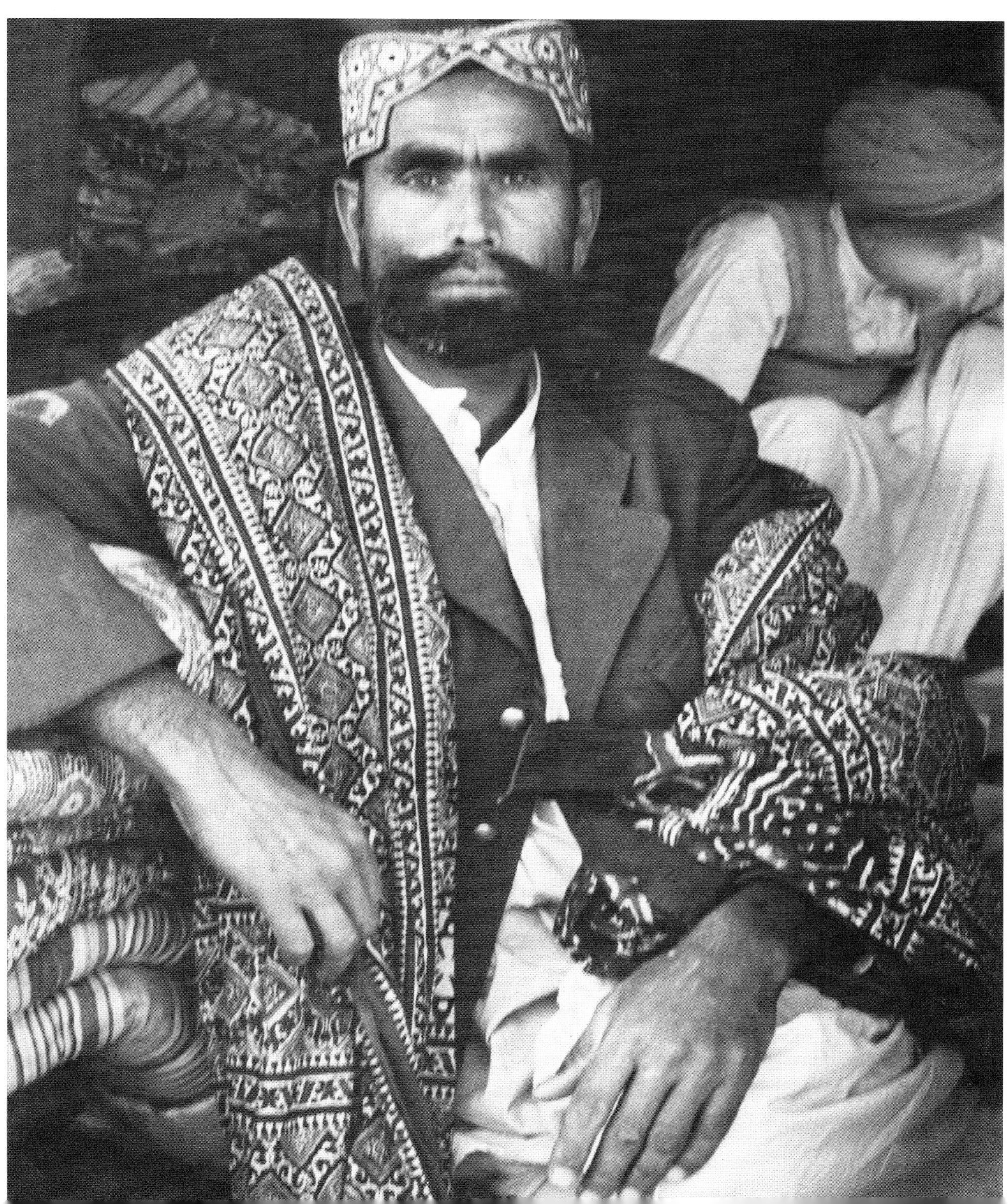

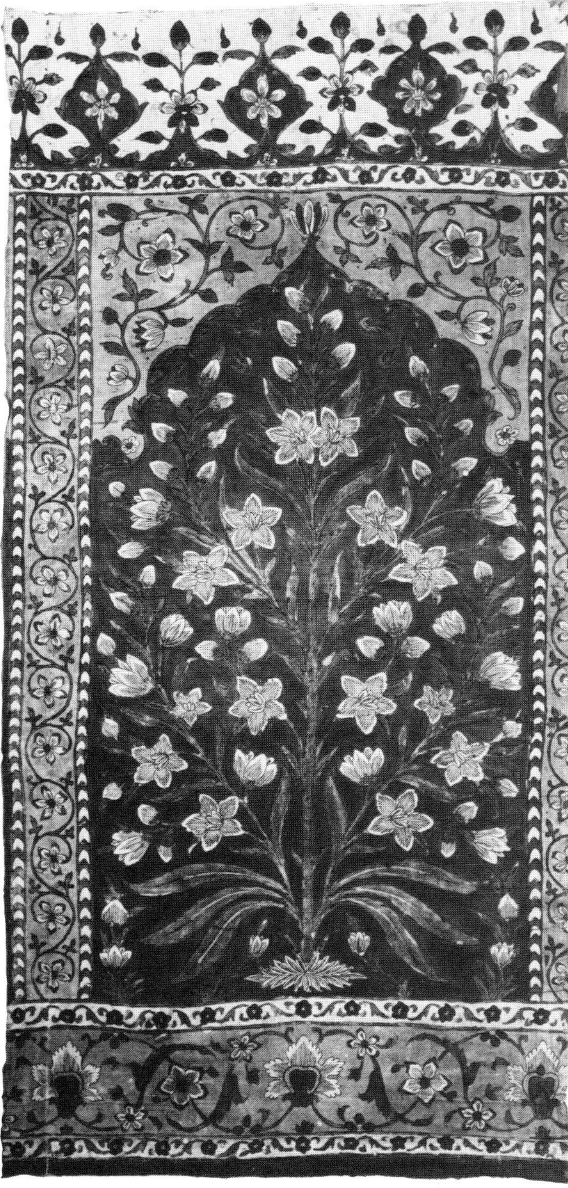

Fig. 37. (Above) **Kanat** (tent hanging), Rajasthan, 19th century. Cotton; woven; hand painted, direct and with mordant; resist dyed; indigo dyed; 2 yd. 16 in. (2.24m) × 1 yd. 5½ in. (1.05m); 58.2-90.

Fig. 38. (Right) **Pichhavai** (temple cloth), Nathadwara, Udaipur district, late 19th century. Cotton; woven; painted with pigment; 1 yd. 25¼ in. (1.55m) × 1 yd. 18⅝ in. (1.38m); 66.61-36.

Clay resists do not fully penetrate the cloth allowing printing of a sharp, clear image on both sides.

A Rajasthani textile that combines mordant dyeing, indigo dyeing, and use of resists with the additional element of painting is the *kanat.* This type of tent hanging is one of a series of panels that were used by Mughal courts to create temporary encampments. In the *kanat* illustrated in Figure 37, black outlines of leaves, vines, and borders were painted by hand with a solution of iron salts, and dark red outlines of flowers were painted with alum. The dark background and flower petals are also red, but the lighter shade of red in these areas required a different mix of the alum mordant. After dyeing in a madder dye bath for red, all of the black and red areas and those to remain white were brushed with resist and immersion dyed a light tannish gold color. Additional resist was applied, and overdyeing, probably with indigo, produced dark green in the leaves, vines, and borders. The *mihrab,* or prayer niche, containing a flowering plant, and the scroll-like vines and stylized flowers of the borders are motifs commonly seen on *kanats.* The top band of this tent hanging is a decorative interpretation of the *kanguri,* the uppermost sculptural element of a *kila* (fortress), a distinctive feature of the Rajasthani landscape.

Painted Textiles

The *pichhavai* temple cloth of the *Vallabhacharya* sect of Nathadwara is a cotton pigment painted textile. This sect worships Shri Nathji, a manifestation of Krishna as Govardhan, who lifted the mountain of Govardhana to shelter his cowherd friends from the torrential rains of the god Indra. Shri Nathji's image is installed in a *haveli* ("palatial mansion"), which is a large town house with several inner courtyards. All the furnishings of the shrine are draped with decorative cloth hangings which create an atmosphere of splendor. This atmosphere is in contrast to other Hindu temples in which the outer walls are decorated while the inner sanctum is small, sparse, and dimly lit. Worship includes the ritual bathing, dressing, and feeding of Shri Nathji at prescribed times throughout the day.

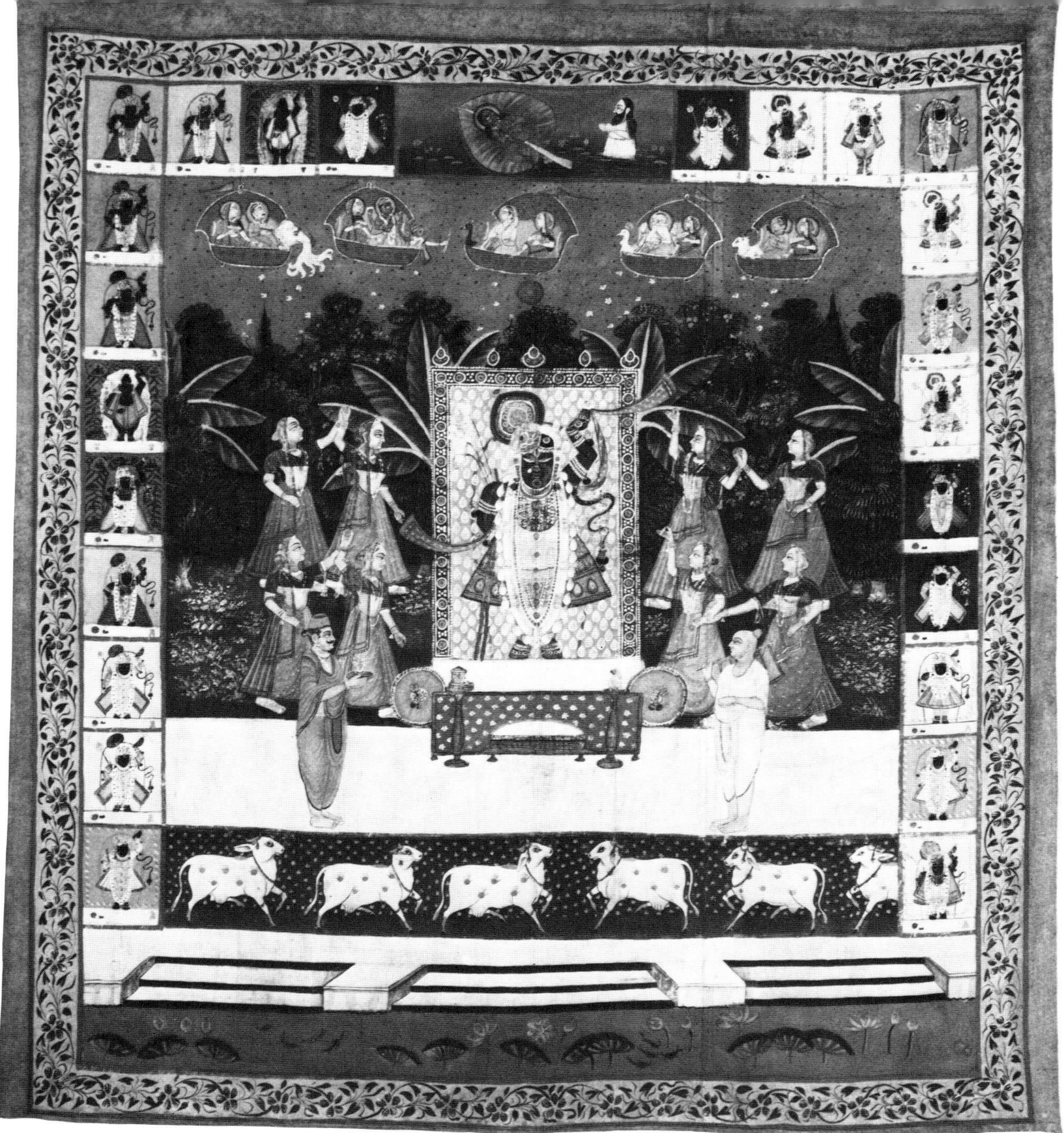

The *pichhavai* (from *pichha* "the back") is the cloth placed behind the image and is the most important hanging in a set of temple cloths. A large central image of Shri Nathji dominates the *pichhavai* (Fig. 38). He is surrounded by attendants and worshippers wearing Rajasthani regional dress. Four gods of the Hindu pantheon in their celestial chariots observe from above. Each of the twenty-four panels typically enclosing a *pichhavai* depicts Shri Nathji resplendent in garments representing twenty-four different festivals of importance to the sect.

These pigment painted textiles differ from those painted with dyes in that the pigment does not penetrate the fibers but rests on the surface of the fabric as in a painting.

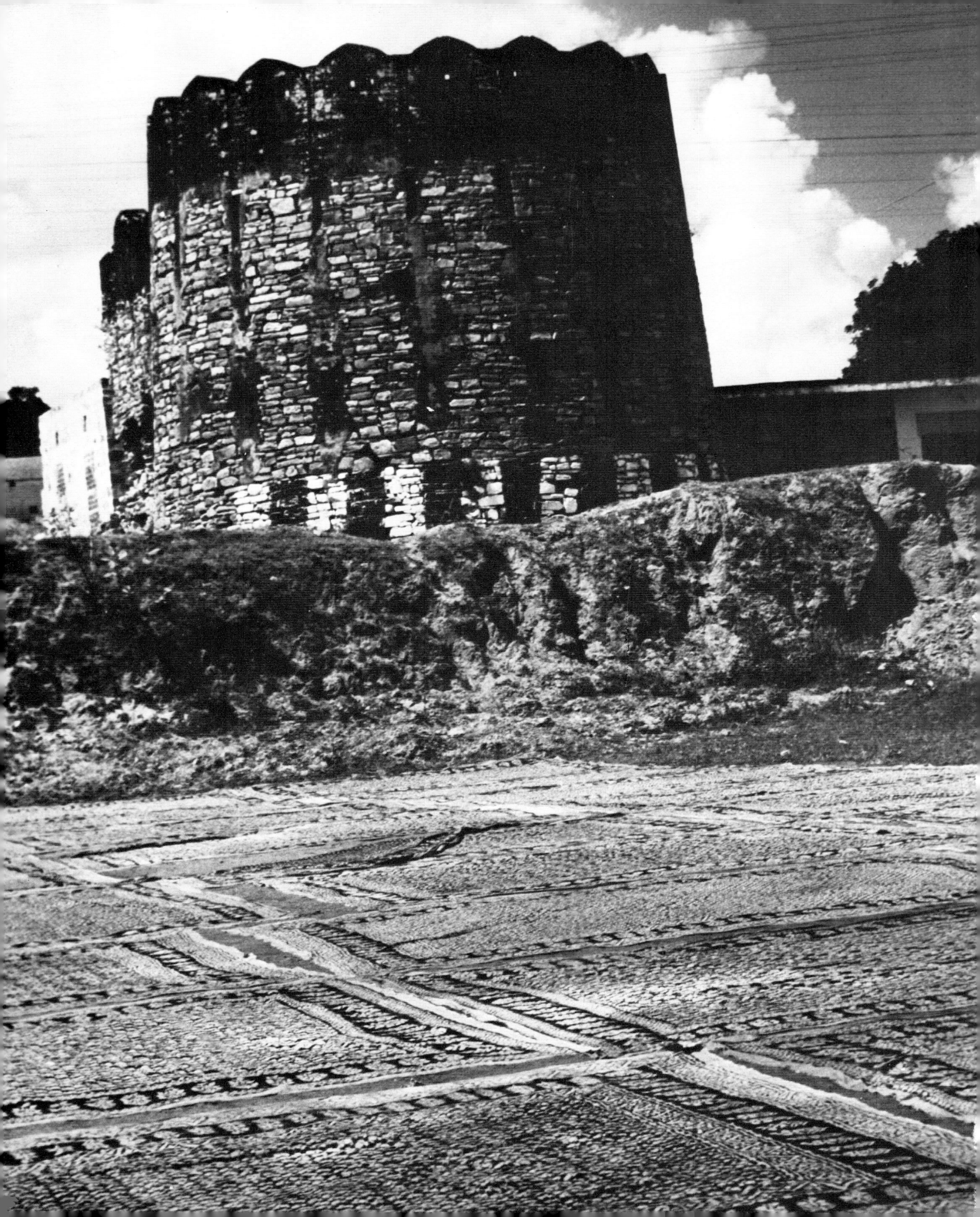

GUJARAT

Gujarat, a small western state of India, is bordered to the north by Rajasthan and to the south by Maharashtra. Its western boundaries are created by the Rann of Kutch, a salt marsh wasteland, and the Arabian Sea. Gujaratis have been involved with maritime trade, apparently since the ancient times of the Indus civilization. Historically, the ports of Cambay, Broach, and Surat were centers of trade with the Middle East and later with Europe. In contrast to these urban ports of trade, rural Gujarat, especially Saurashtra and Kutch in their relative physical isolation, remained enmeshed in many traditions and group identities which have retained integrity down to the present day.

Of the four states discussed in this catalogue, Gujarat produces textiles of cotton, silk, and wool with the greatest variety of techniques. Orissa, Andhra Pradesh, and Gujarat all have strong ikat traditions; Gurarati ikat, however, has the longest recorded history. Resist dyed textiles include not only ikat but also wax or paste resists applied with blocks, and *bandhana.* Additional surface decoration such as embroidery and mirror embroidery is often combined with resist dyed techniques. Within the major category of hand printed textiles are the techniques of mordant printing and dyeing, tinsel printing, and the direct application of color. Production and use of these textiles is widely dispersed throughout Gujarat.

Textiles produced in an urban context such as Ahmedabad, Gujarat's former capital and India's sixth largest city, are representative of the continuing traditions of printing and resist dyeing in Gujarat. Ahmedabad includes a great diversity of peoples, costumes, and cultures, and it serves as a crossroad of commerce, transportation, and agriculture. Inhabitants of the outlying, more remote parts of Gujarat routinely come into Ahmedabad for essentials, adding to the richness of the visual scene. Another facet of Ahmedabad's diversity is its architecture. Twentieth-century buildings of concrete and brick by Doshi, Le Corbusier, and Louis Kahn coexist beside twelfth- and fifteenth-century mosques and temples of carved sandstone and marble. In the sixteenth century Ahmedabad was completely enclosed by a thick wall with twelve main gates. Today, encircled by textile factories, the remaining gates continue to be prominent landmarks of the dense old city built along the right bank of the Sabarmati River (Fig. 39).

Fig. 39. Part of the original sixteenth century wall remains along the bank of the Sabarmati River, which has for centuries been used for washing and drying textiles.

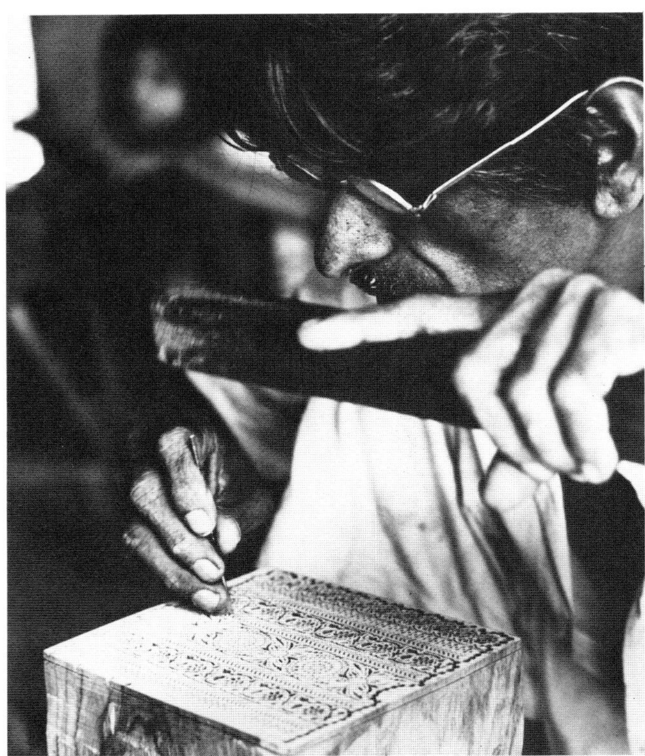

Fig. 40. An assistant at the block making workshop in Pethapur carefully defines the design as outlined by the bow drill. He cuts the block design in high relief, approximately ¼ in.

Hand Block Printing

In Pethapur, a Gujarati village between Ahmedabad and Patan, the craft of wood block making is practiced today by one master craftsman with assistants and six apprentices who are subsidized by the government and the All India Handicraft Board. With no son to inherit his skills as tradition would dictate, Maneklal Gujjar, the master craftsman, has chosen to train his daughter as an apprentice.

Wood is purchased from a forest in Gujarat south of Ahmedabad. The wood, called *sag*, (referred to as teak) is cut into rounds and stored for one year in a cool place under the house. The wood is then cut into blocks of various sizes four to five inches thick. The first step in preparation is leveling and sanding to create a smooth work surface and an even polish and patina to the wood. Squared and polished, the surface receives a coating of plaster to enable the design to be read more clearly. The master craftsman then draws the design on paper and transfers the design to the block using a bow drill which perforates the outlines of the paper pattern. Small chisels are used to cut the design in fairly high relief (Fig. 40). After the design is completed, the handle is carved into the back. The master craftsman draws the design on paper which may take up to two days; his apprentices and assistants prepare and carve the blocks, each requiring up to one week. Today the blocks are prepared on commission for markets all over India including Ahmedabad, Bombay, Delhi, and Varanasi. In the past the entire process, including the printing onto cloth, was done in Pethapur by other specialized groups.

Block printing represents perhaps the most widely practiced textile process in India today and incorporates several different techniques in its application. Blocks are used extensively in Gujarat, Rajasthan, and Andhra Pradesh to apply mordants and resists and to apply color directly to cloth. In the mordant printing technique as practiced in Gujarat, a mordant such as alum is first stamped onto the cloth. *Haldi* (turmeric) is often added as a fugitive colorant to the clear alum to facilitate registration. A fermented solution of iron scraps and *jagri* (brown palm sugar) is boiled down to form a paste. This paste is block printed onto a premordanted cloth, creating a permanent black. The cloth is then immersed in a red dye bath. *Saranguy* (*Morinda citrifolia*) was commonly used in western India to produce reds until the turn of the century; synthetic alizarin is now used. *Chay* (*Oldenlandia umbellata*) was and still is used on the eastern coast. After dyeing and rinsing, the unmordanted areas remain a cream or tan, a characteristic of this mordant technique.

Figure 41 illustrates a mordant printed sari from Ahmedabad in deep red, black, and tan. Registration lines or shadows where blocks meet are clearly visible on this sari. Two blocks used repetitively build up a patterned field of diagonal *chauks* (crosses, squares, or intersections). Apparent is the repeated use of several blocks to create the bands of the *pallu*. The bands of *butas* (large floral designs) are created with a ground stamp for the deep red and a figure stamp for the black floral outlining.

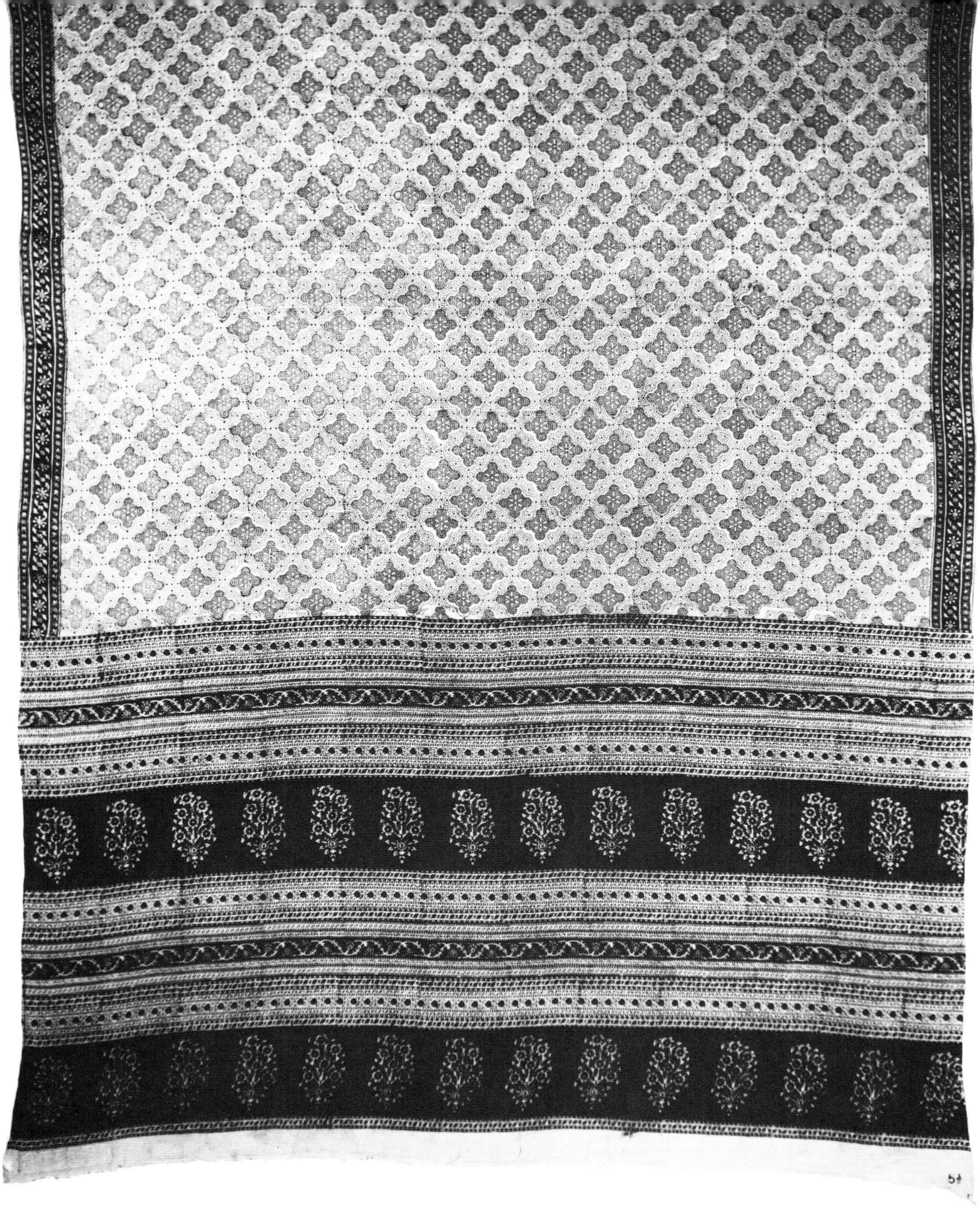

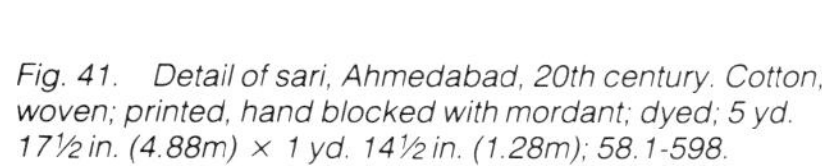

Fig. 41. Detail of sari, Ahmedabad, 20th century. Cotton; woven; printed, hand blocked with mordant; dyed; 5 yd. 17½ in. (4.88m) × 1 yd. 14½ in. (1.28m); 58.1-598.

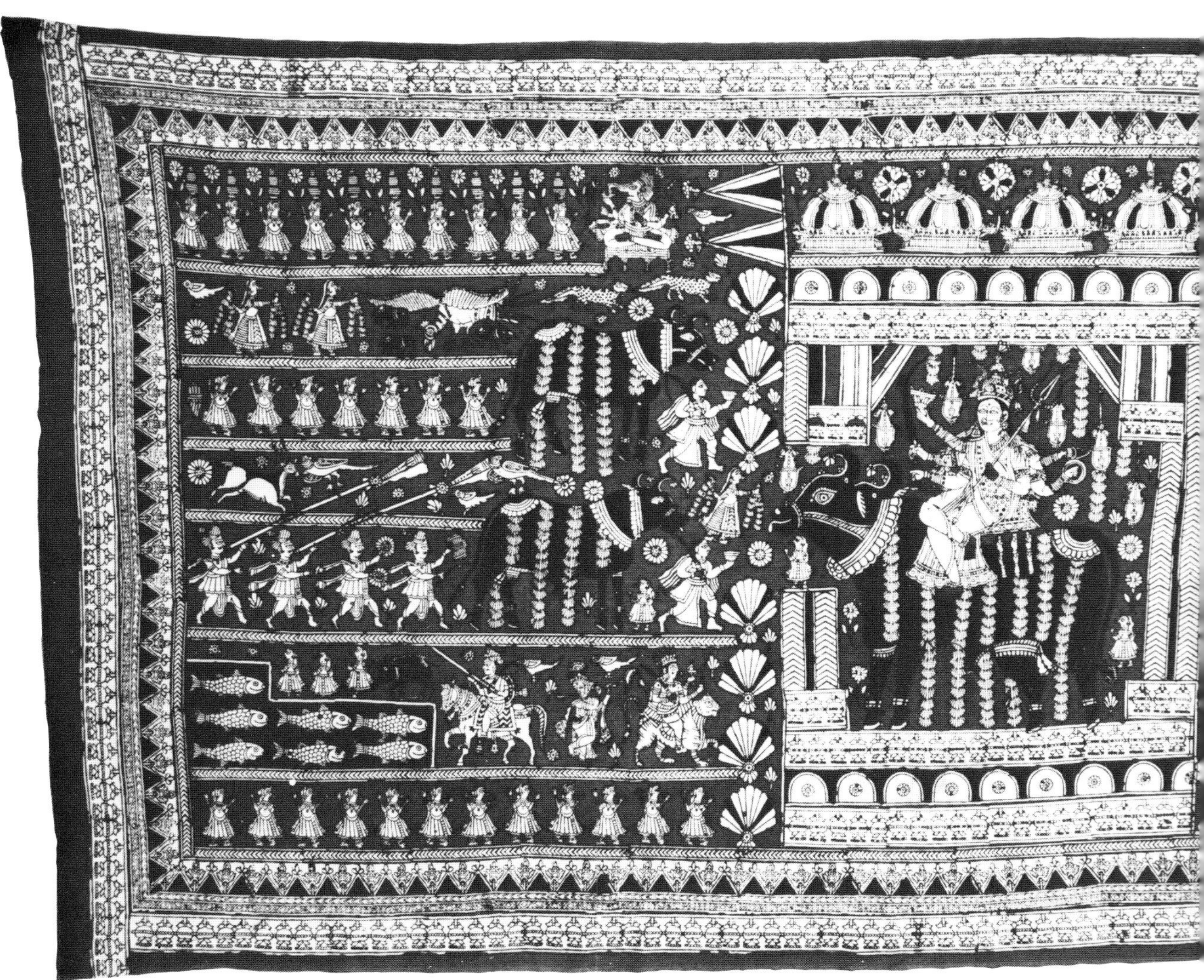

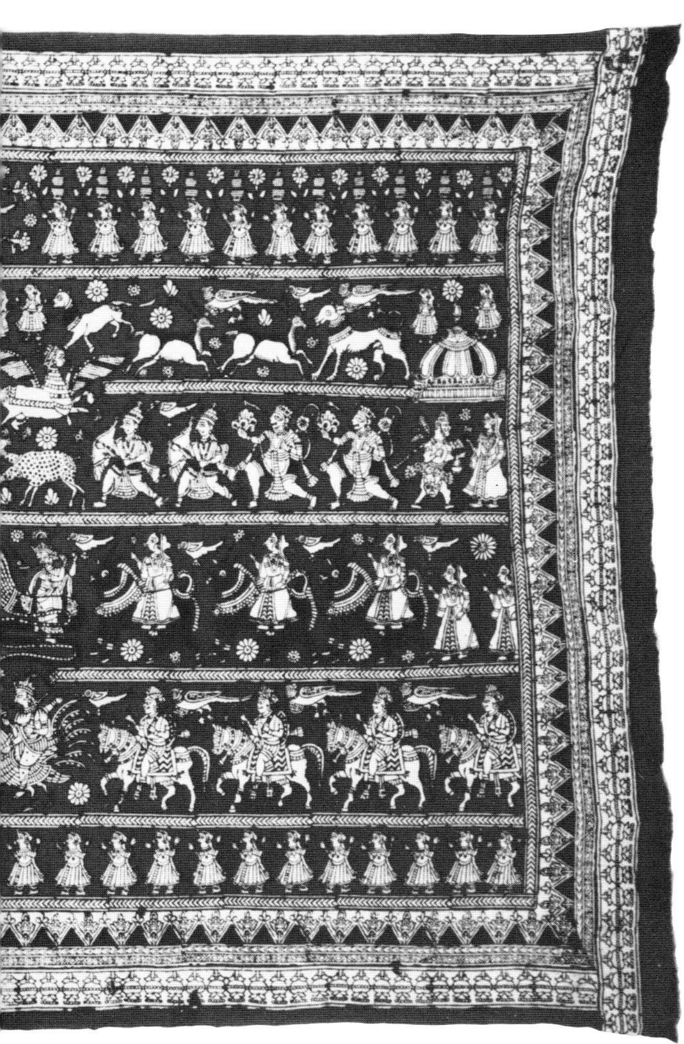

Fig. 42. **Mata Pachedi** *(temple cloth), Ahmedabad, 20th century (1957). Cotton; woven; printed, hand blocked with mordant; painted with mordant; 2 yd. 33½ in. (2.68m) × 1 yd. 18¼ in. (1.38m); 58.2-79.*

Another Ahmedabad textile hand blocked with mordants is the *Mata Pachedi*, a temple cloth for the *Mata*, or Mother Goddess. Produced by families of semi-nomadic Vaghries, these cloths serve as temporary and portable temples for worship of the *Mata*, reflecting the nomadic origins of these people. Cloths known as *Mata Chandarvo* are also prepared to serve as the ceiling or top of the temple. They are readily distinguished from the *Pachedis* by their square format, larger size, and large central circular motif.

Worship of the Mother Goddess is one of India's most ancient cults and varies from region to region all over the country. The *Mata* represents the creative and the destructive forces of the universe, and her hand and foot are painted red or black to suggest her dark and destructive nature. The *Mata,* or mother, the centrally placed, most prominent figure, is presented in Figure 42 in one of her seven manifestations, that of the goddess Bhadrakali mounted on a black buffalo. The *Mata Pachedi's* role as a *katha,* or visual storytelling, highlights the compelling and powerful nature of the textile.

The *Mata Pachedi* is crowded with architectural details that further evoke the image of a temple and that are printed in sequence ceremonially preparing a space for the *Mata.* A series of temple bells which enclose the entire textile is the first detail to be printed; next is the inner temple crowned with four Gujarati-style domes. The textile is then ready to receive the *Mata,* whose image is block printed inside her temple. Ganesha, the elephant-headed god, is traditionally placed in the upper left. All figures in the rows on the left side of the *Mata's* temple face toward her, bearing offerings and gifts. Rows of figures on the right side of the temple relate a Krishna legend and an episode from the *Ramayana,* including the figures of Rama, Lakshman, Hanuman, Sita, and Ravana. Outside rows on both right and left depict women devotees dressed in typical Gujarati clothing, the *odhani* and *ghaghara.* The background areas are red, having been painted with an alum mordant before dyeing. All other outlines and figures are black and were block printed or painted with a solution of iron salts.

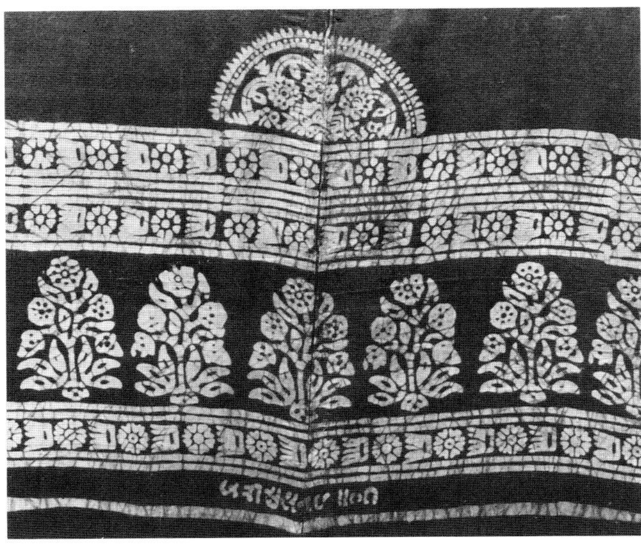

Fig. 43. Detail of **odhani**, *Saurashtra, early 20th century. Silk; woven, satin weave; resist dyed; printed, hand blocked with wax or paste resist; indigo dyed; 4 yd. 23½ in. (4.26m) × 1 yd. 19 in. (1.4m); 58.2-80.*

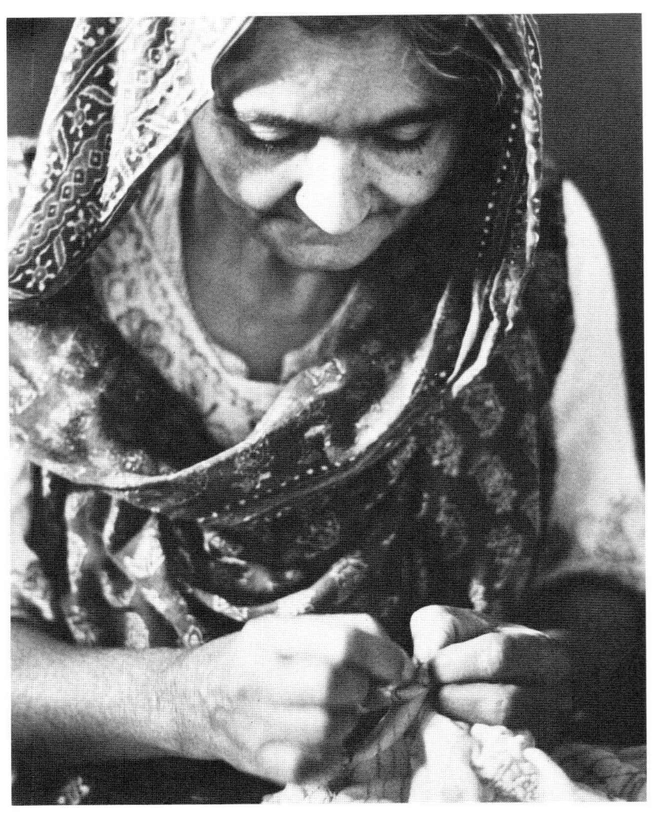

Resist Dyeing

Wax, paste, and clay slip are all used in Gujarat as resists and may be applied with a printing block. The *odhanis,* commonly worn in Kutch and Saurashtra, are good examples of this technique. The resist used in the silk *odhani* in Figure 43 appears to be wax, which gives a characteristic crackling effect. The design in this *odhani* is magenta, and the background is vat dyed indigo blue. Floral motifs alternate with *pad,* the footprint of God, a religious symbol commonly seen in Indian textiles. Resist has also been applied with a brush in the inscription in the central bottom of the border. Inscriptions indicating ownership or codes developed by craftsmen are often seen in Gujarati textiles.

Bandhana

The *bandhana* technique in Gujarat is utilized in festive, ceremonial, and everyday clothing. The cloth bazaar in the town of Bhuj, Kutch district, is colorfully lined with small stalls displaying intricately tied fabrics with brightly dyed patterns. It is common to buy *bandhana* pieces still folded and tied with only the outer corner opened to assure the buyer that the product was hand knotted. Inside, in the relative coolness of the shops, men tie cotton cloths. Women also tie the cloth, working in the houses on narrow lanes off the main streets of the bazaar (Fig. 44).

A red wedding sari, called *gharchola,* is a ceremonial garment in which *bandhana* figures appear in a woven grid of gold (Fig. 45). Because of its intended use as a wedding sari, the *gharchola* contains the auspicious elephant and other symbols of good fortune. The grid

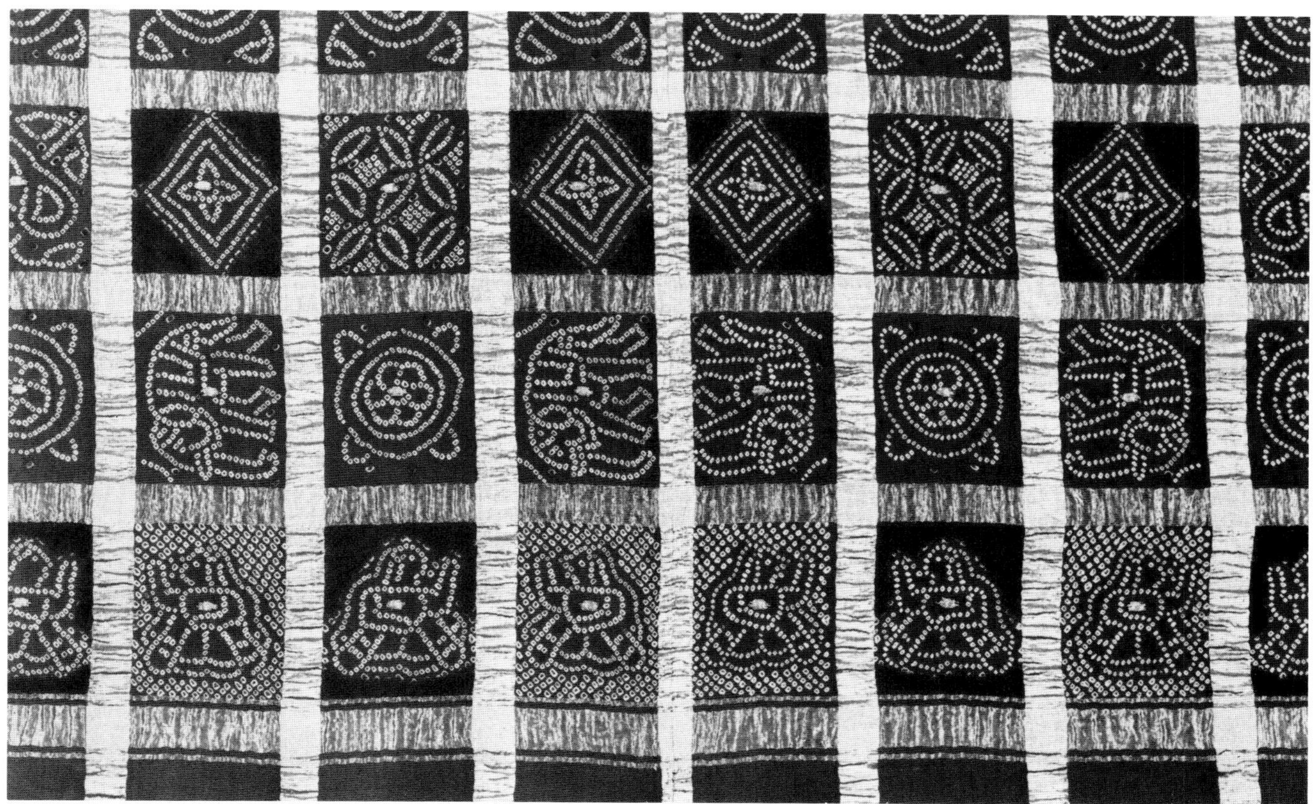

pattern created by *chauks* may be either diagonal or rectangular and is known as *chaukhana*. In this *gharchola* a yellow cloth with the woven grid of gold is folded in half selvedge to selvedge before tying begins. The tied design results in a symmetrical mirror image as seen in the center of the cloth. Designs are often ruled out or stamped on with wooden blocks in a fugitive material, such as chalk or charcoal, to indicate outlines for tying. Design areas to remain yellow in the cloth are pinched up into small dots and bound tightly with a continuous thread. Areas where green is desired are first brushed with color and then resisted with ties to protect them from the red dye bath.

Fig. 44. (Center) Muslim woman in Bhuj, Kutch district, binding off areas, outlined in chalk, with a continuous string as the second step in the **bandhana** *process.*

Fig. 45. (Above) Detail of **gharchola**, *Bhuj, Kutch district, 20th century. The* **gharchola's** *golden grid pattern creates 4 in. rectangles, each containing a* **bandhana** *motif. The facing elephants indicate the lateral fold of the cloth producing this mirror image. The bottom row of women represents devotees. Cotton; woven, plaid with gold; supplementary weft patterning in gold; resist dyed,* **bandhana**; *painted; 5 yd. 4½ in. (4.56m) × 1 yd. 14 in. (1.27m); 58.1-446.*

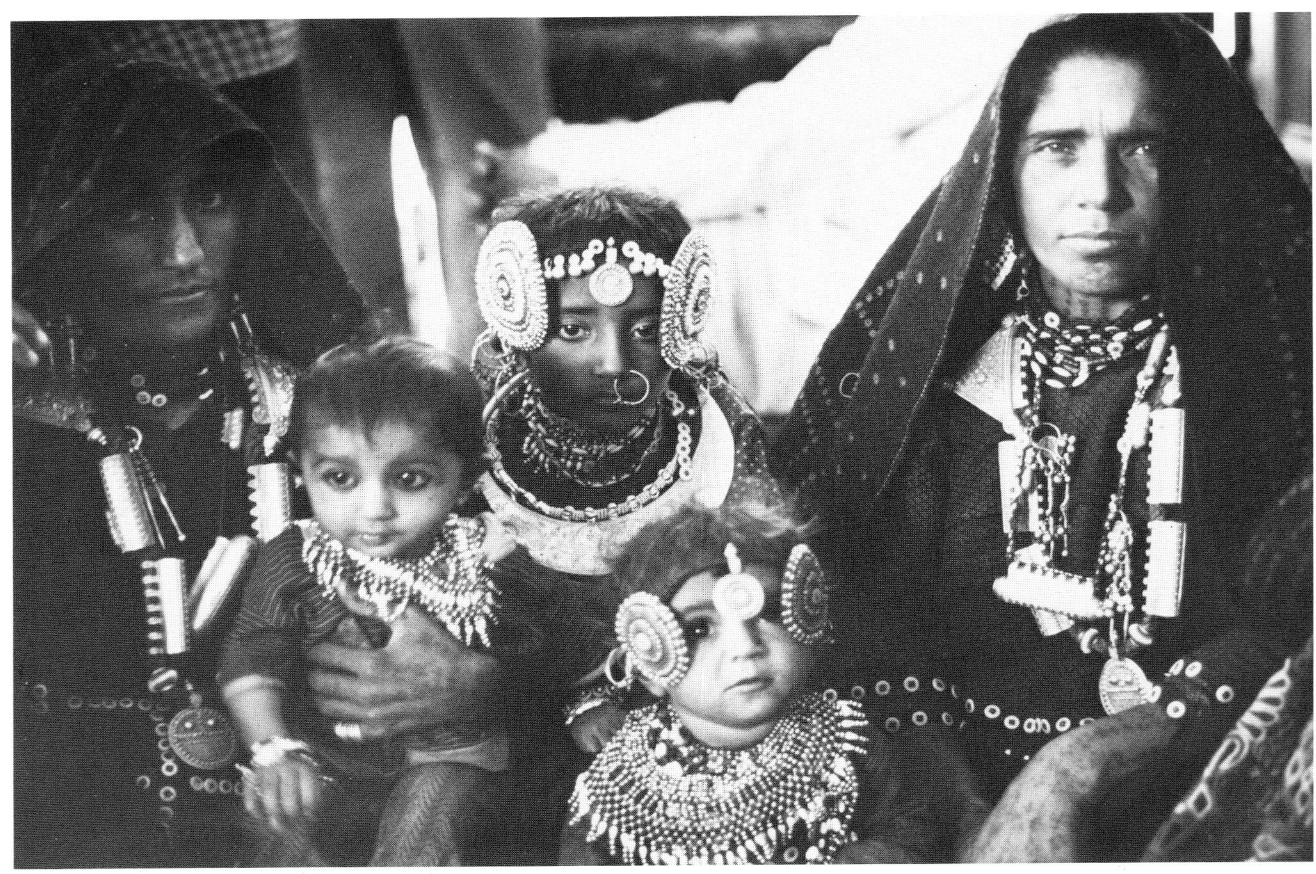

*Fig. 46. The Rabaris, a pastoral group which inhabits the Kutch, have a very distinctive costume. The women wear heavy dark wool **odhanis** with tie dyed geometric patterning. Their **ghagharas** are richly embroidered. The **bandhana** designs of the **odhanis** are repeated in their silver jewelry and especially in the tatooing of their neck and hands.*

Hindu women's traditional garments in Kutch and Saurashtra are the *odhani* and the *ghaghara*. *Odhanis* from Gujarat and Rajasthan are frequently tie dyed. Their composition, whether a plain field or patterned, contains a central medallion or several smaller ones enclosed by intricate and informative bands of plangi. *Bandhana* is used on *odhanis* of cotton, silk, and wool, and further surface decoration such as embroidery and mirror embroidery is favored both by Hindu and by Muslim women in Kutch (Fig. 46).

Although Indian women generally have retained their traditional regional garments longer than men, the men of Gujarat, especially of Kutch and Saurashtra, continue to wear *kamri,* a jacket with side tie closures, and either *salwar,* trousers with a drawstring waist, or a shorter variation of the *dhoti,* an unstitched draped garment. *Kamblas* (shoulder cloths), of coarse wool with supplementary weft patterning, parallel the woman's *odhani* in their construction. They are made of two loom-width panels of cloth decoratively joined in the center. Men's clothing is most often white, appropriate for Gujarat's dry and relentlessly hot days (Fig. 47).

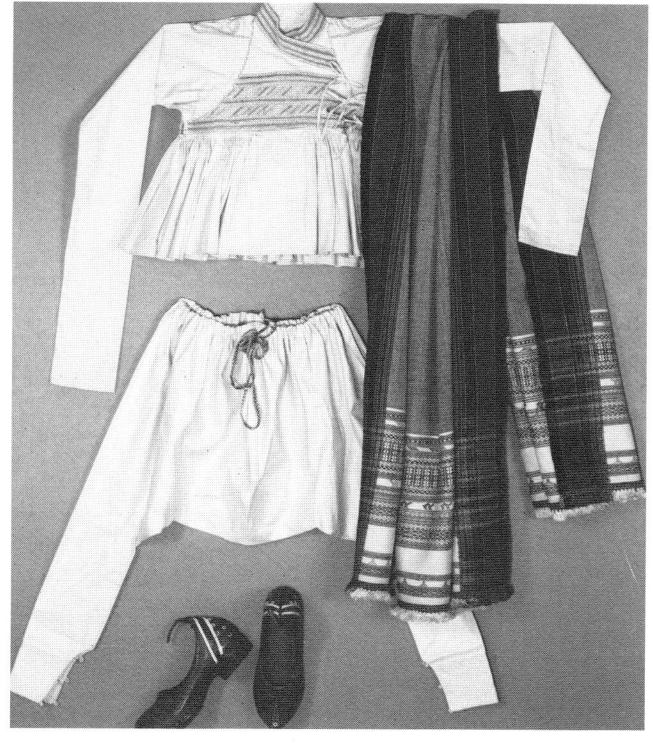

Fig. 47. The man's costume worn both in Kutch and in Kathiawar is a visual counterpoint to the dark costume of the Rabari women. The jacket and pants are most often white. The jacket is embroidered by hand or machine on both the front and back panels. ***Kamri*** *(man's jacket), Rajkot, Rajkot district, Kathiawar, 58.1-360, t2;* ***salwar*** *(man's trousers), 58.1-360, t1;* ***kambla*** *(blanket), 58.1-224; man's shoes, leather, 58.2-210, m1 & m2.*

Double Ikat Patola

Historically created in an urban context, the *patola* (*patolu,* singular) are the only double ikat textiles produced in Gujarat. Patan, Cambay, Surat, and Ahmedabad were once *patola* weaving centers; in the nineteenth century over seven hundred households were involved in *patola* production in Patan alone. Today in Gujarat only two extended families, in Patan, are still producing *patola. Patola* are historically significant for their ceremonial and religious usage and as important trade items especially with the Indonesian Archipelago. Continuation of the traditional ceremonial use is maintained today in Gujarat on a limited scale. In contrast to the volume of hand production of many contemporary textiles for recognized markets, *patola* are now woven in small quantities for commisson only. The *patolu* combines high technical artistry, a richness of design motifs, and great ceremonial significance.

Traditionally labeled a wedding sari, the *patolu* should more appropriately be called a ceremonial sari. The specific ceremonial use varies with the religious group or caste. In the past, mothers of the bridal couple and other female relatives of the bride in a Gujarati wedding might have worn their *patola* rather than the bride herself wearing one. Today, however, the *patolu* is considered a major part of the bride's dowry by some groups in Gujarat. The groom may also wear the *patolu* as a shoulder cloth. Hindus, Jains, and Bohra Muslims celebrate the seventh month of a woman's pregnancy with a ceremony called *Simanta,* in which a pregnant woman sits cross-legged on the floor on a *patolu* while she receives gifts. *Patola* may be used as temple hangings, shrouds, animal coverings, or as a canopy during the worship of the Mother Goddess. There is healing power associated with the burned ashes of *patola* fragments.

Of critical importance to the success of a *patolu* is the preparation of the warp and weft for the double ikat. Separate warps are prepared for the main field and the borders. Currently, saris are forty-eight-and-one-half inches in width. As approximately fifty ends per inch are used, this translates into preparation of 2,500 to 2,800 warp threads, each of which must be kept in exact relationship to its neighboring threads. If a thread becomes crossed or moved, it will be apparent in the final product. A warp of twenty yards is prepared; from this three saris are woven. Warps are grouped in bundles composed of fourteen groups of twelve threads each. After the warp is removed from the warping pegs, it is folded laterally to create six layers. This step allows the tying of like patterns in three saris simultaneously. This folding technique also explains the occurrence of mirror patterning as is easily

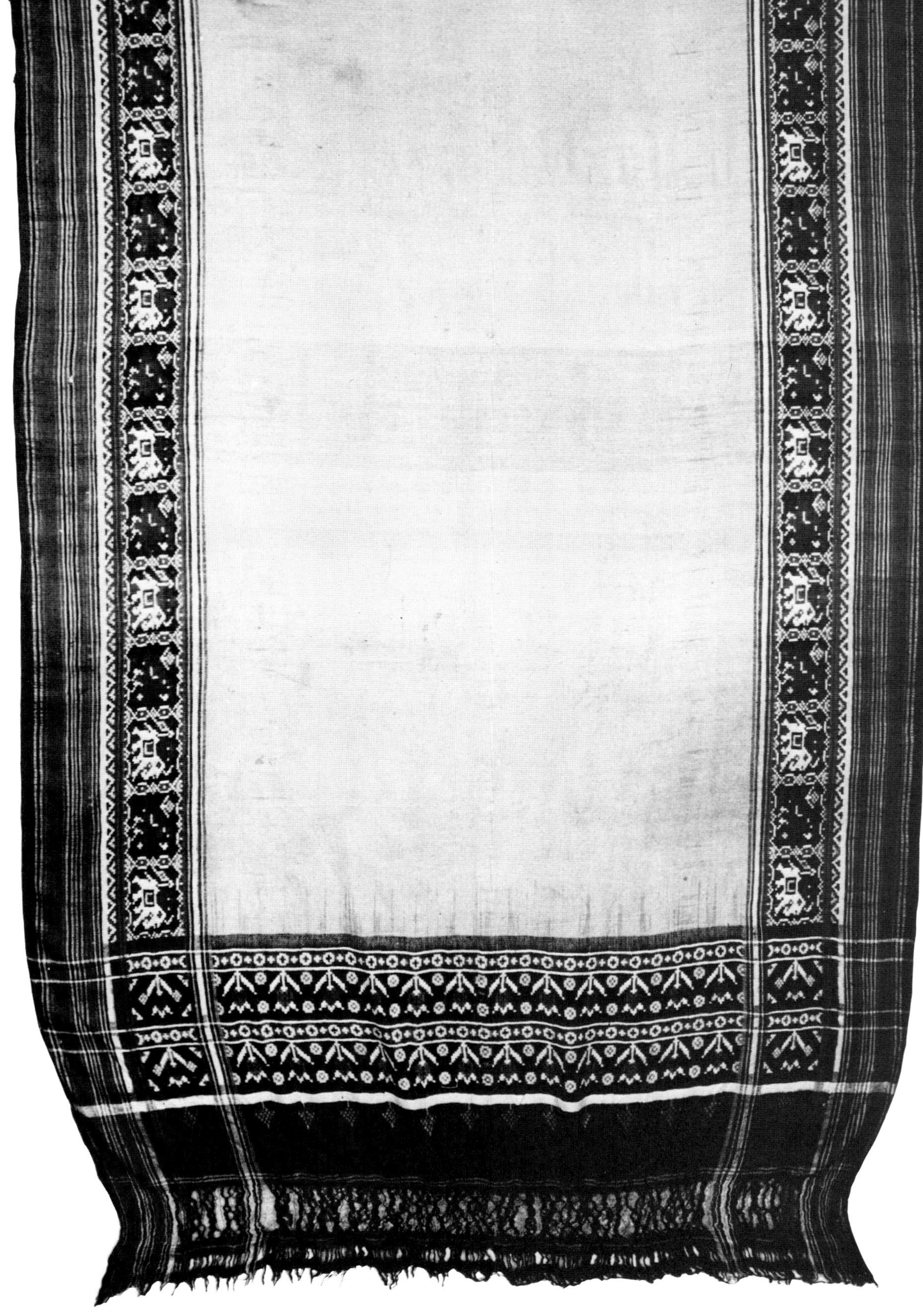

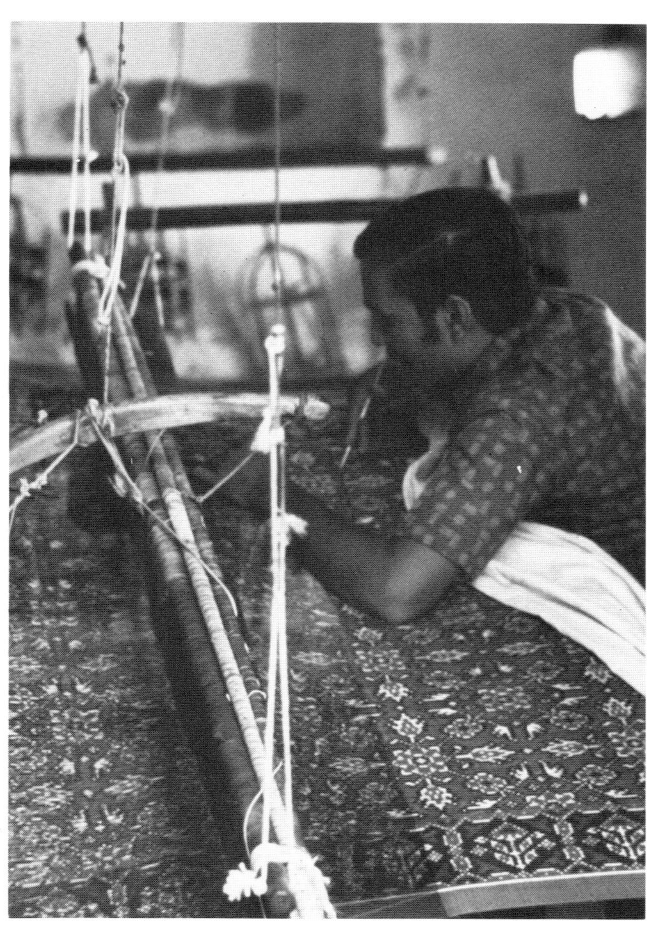

Fig. 48. (Left) Detail of **chir bhat** (plain design) **patolu** sari, late 19th century. Silk and gold; woven, resist dyed, double ikat; 4 yd. (3.66m) × 1 yd. 17 in. (1.35m); 58.2-47.

Fig. 49. (Above) The weavers in Patan carefully manipulate each warp and weft with a metal stylus as the weaving proceeds to realign any slippage or shifting in the pattern. This exacting process greatly increases the weaving time but allows for greater clarity and precision of design. The further registering of the design with a stylus is not used by any other ikat weavers in India.

seen in the center of the sari border in Figure 48 where a repeated red parrot occurs. The warps are vertically marked at one-centimeter intervals with charcoal and the areas to be resisted are wrapped tightly and held in place with a half hitch. As *patola* saris are double ikat, a similar process must be followed when preparing the weft threads. Separate wefts are prepared for the main field and *pallu,* and several layers are resist tied simultaneously. These resisted warp and weft threads must meet precisely to create a clear double ikat pattern. The weaver is able to manipulate the threads on the loom with a small metal stylus, as shown in Figure 49, to achieve some additional realignment, but the primary registration must occur in the actual tying process.

A distinctive feature of the *patolu* sari is the *counter pallu* which is almost equal in width to the *pallu.* The double ikat patterning of the *pallu* and *counter pallu* is identical. The *pallu* is identified by an additional woven area which often contains a band of gold weft. *Patola* have either patterned or plain central fields enclosed by longitudinal borders and the *pallu* and *counter pallu.* The double ikat patterning of the central patterned field is arranged in either a rectangular or diamond grid system (*chauk*) as seen in other Gujarati textiles, such as the *gharchola* illustrated in Figure 45, and the sari from Ahmedabad in Figure 41. *Patola* intended for use in India are totally of silk. Deep red is the predominant color with the motifs in white, yellow, yellow green, blue green, and reddish black. The borders on many *patola* feature repeating parrots and elephants. Fifty-three motifs found in the central field of *patola* saris have been identified and grouped into seven major categories by the late Alfred Bühler and Eberhard Fischer in their definitive study, *The Patola of Gujarat* (Basle: Museum of Ethnography, 1979). One category is devoted to the double ikat fabrics woven for *cholis.* Contemporary motifs and adaptations of traditional motifs comprise the second category. The remaining five categories are traditional designs with either plain or patterned fields.

The third major grouping of *patola* are those called *chir bhat* (plain design). These have a monochromatic field which is either red, grayed gold, or brilliant orange-gold (see Fig. 48). The double ikat borders are alternating elephants and red parrots. The double ikat motifs in the *pallu* and *counter pallu* are double bands of stylized floral motifs which frame and contrast with the richly colored plain field.

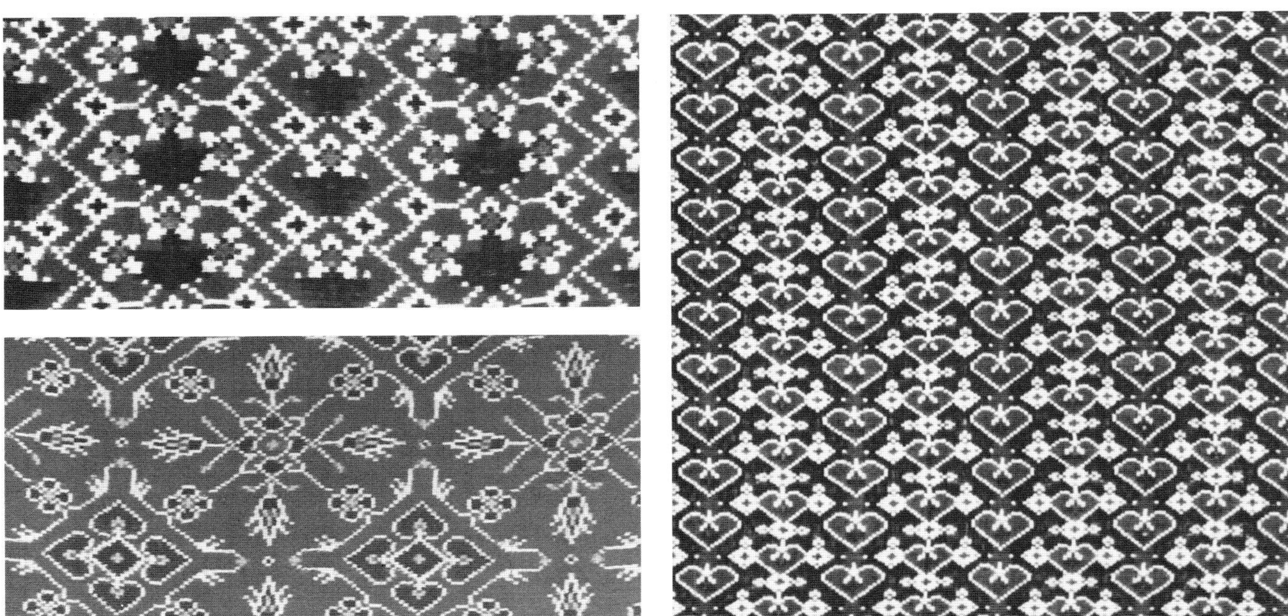

Fig. 51. (Top) ***Phul bhat*** *(field of flowers design)* ***patolu*** *sari fragment, late 19th century. Silk; woven; resist dyed, double ikat; 18½ in. (.67m) × 17 in. (.43m); 58.2-35.*

Fig. 52. (Bottom) ***Chhabadi bhat*** *(design of circles or baskets containing flowers)* ***patolu*** *sari fragment, 19th century. Silk; woven; resist dyed, double ikat; 22¼ in. (.565m) × 30 in. (.51m); 58.2-45.*

The most frequent patterned design category is the repetition of a single leaf motif called *pan bhat* (leaf design). The heart-shaped leaf depicted is that of the *pan* or sacred pipal tree (Fig. 50). Often the *pan bhat patolu* sari had Gujarati inscriptions written on the *pallu.* Ownership of these saris, as established by translations, has included groups such as the Nagar Brahmans and the Lohana merchants of Saurashtra, the Anavil Brahmans of Surat, and the Bhatia merchants of Kutch.

Another major category is that of floral patterned fields. *Phul bhat* (field of flowers design) is a stepped rectangular arrangement of rows of baskets containing a single flower enclosed by diamonds (*chauks*) al-

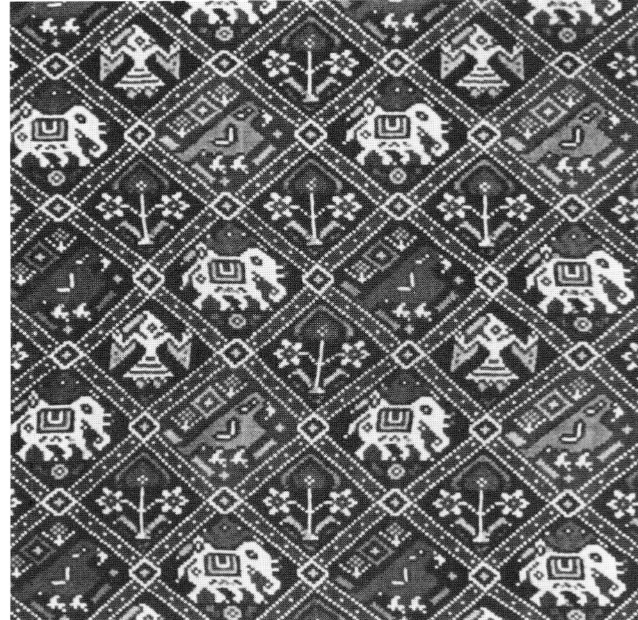

Fig. 50. (Top) Detail of ***pan bhat*** *(leaf design)* ***patolu*** *sari, late 19th century. Silk and gold; woven; resist dyed, double ikat; 4 yd. 1½ in. (3.7m) × 1 yd. 14½ in. (1.28m); 58.2-32.*

Fig. 53. (Bottom) Detail of ***nari kunjar popat phul bhat*** *(girl, elephant, parrot, flower design)* ***patolu*** *sari, late 19th century. Silk and gold; woven; resist dyed, double ikat; 4 yd. 14½ in. (4.03m) × 1 yd. 17 in. (1.35m); 58.2-39.*

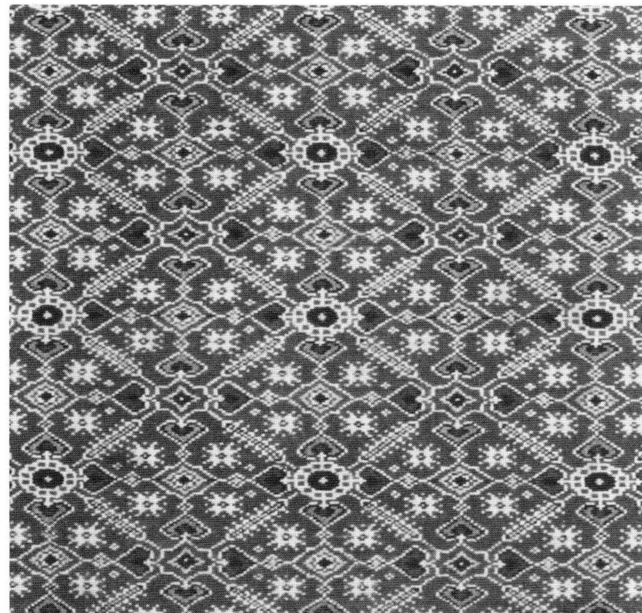

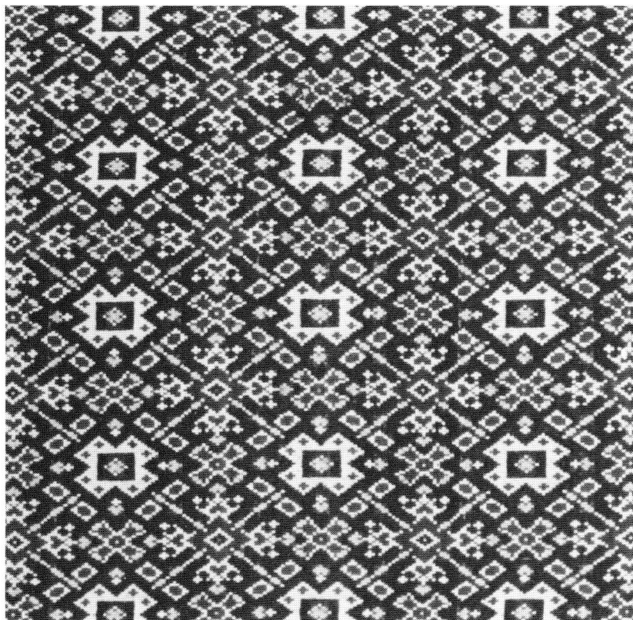

Fig. 54. (Top) Detail of **Vohra gaji bhat** *(design preferred by Bohra Muslims)* **patolu** *sari, late 19th century. Silk and gold; woven; resist dyed, double ikat; 4 yd. 34 in. (4.52m) × 1 yd. 8½ in. (1.13m); 58.2-41.*

Fig. 55. (Bottom) Detail of **ratan chauk bhat** *(jeweled diamond design)* **patolu** *sari, late 19th century. Silk and gold; woven; resist dyed, double ikat; 3 yd. 33½ in. (3.6m) × 1 yd. 15½ in. (1.31m); 58.2-29.*

ternating with baskets of three flowers contained by hexagons (Fig. 51). Some of the *phul bhat patola* were popular export items in Java and Bali. In Ahmedabad, a Jain bride traditionally received this floral designed sari as a wedding gift from her maternal uncle. *Chhabadi bhat* (a circle or basket containing flowers) is a more stylized floral arrangement and was used both locally, as in the example of an *odhani* for the Anavil Brahman brides of Surat, and for export to Indonesia (Fig. 52).

The sixth major classification of *patola* are the combined floral and animal motifs. Enclosed in an overall diagonal gridwork of *chauks* in Figure 53 are repeating girls, elephants, parrots, and flowers (*nari, kunjar, popat, phul bhat*). Large diamonds enclose two sets of motifs: the first consists of white elephants and green parrots, and the second of white elephants and red parrots. Alternating among these rows are diamonds containing dancing girls and flowers and rows of flowers only. This is the most beloved pattern of the Gujarati people. Nagar Brahmans used the *nari, kunjar, popat, phul bhat patola* as a bridal sari, and it was also presented as gifts to princes and used as elephant blankets for ceremonial rides in southern India. This double ikat pattern made for export to Indonesia would include a lion motif in the diagonal gridwork patterning.

A major grouping of motifs is that of either abstract or geometric motifs arranged in diagonal or rectangular patterning, which may be complemented with plant motifs. A well-known example of abstracted motifs arranged in diagonal patterns is *Vohra gaji bhat* (Fig. 54), a design made for the Bohra Muslims. This complex pattern shows the mixing of common *patola* motifs such as the *pan* leaf with the introduction of the caterpillar-like motifs distinctive to this design. The caterpillar shapes radiate off from the central *pan* leaves to create an overall appearance of diagonal lines. Another distinctive feature of this sari is the treatment of the *pallu.* An extended temple motif in double ikat replaces the more familiar double band of flowering plants. The Bohra Muslims used this sari in the *Simanta* ceremony, marking the seventh month of pregnancy. The arrangement of geometric motifs in a rectangular field is seen in *ratan chauk bhat* (jeweled diamond design) (Fig. 55).

Glossary

Because the Indian terminology used here was derived from a number of Indian languages and often taken from secondary sources, we were unable to maintain a consistency in the use of diacritical marks. We have therefore elected not to use this system. *A Practical Hindi-English Dictionary,* edited by Mahendra Chaturvedi and Dr. Bhola Nath Tiwari (Delhi: National Publishing House, 1975) served as the reference to Hindi spellings.

aba — A stitched, loose fitting upper garment worn by Muslim women of Kutch. The neck, yoke, and edges of the sleeves are richly embroidered.

ajarak — In western India and Pakistan, a process which combines mordant printing, resist-dyeing, and indigo dyeing.

alizarin — The chemical or colorant naturally found in the roots of certain plants such as madder and *chay* which produces a red dye. A synthetic alizarin was produced after 1868 and is commonly used in India. In western India, synthetic alizarin is the primary source for red dyes today.

bandhana, bandhani — From Hindi "to tie or bind." Portions of the fabric are protected from the dye by tying or binding with thread. Also known as plangi.

bichitrapar — Plaid design in Orissan textiles.

buta, buti — A floral motif derived from Persian sources during the Mughal period. A *buta* is a large motif, and a *buti* is a small motif of this type.

chhabadi bhat — The design of a circle or a basket containing flowers in Gujarati *patola.*

chandarvo — A canopy cloth often used along with the *Mata Pachedi* in the worship of the Mother Goddess in Gujarat.

charkha — A spinning wheel.

chauk — A crossing, square; a marketplace.

chaukhana — Gold grid pattern of the *gharchola* sari which is derived from the *chauk,* or square.

chauper — A gameboard, often made of cloth, shaped like a cross. The shape is used as a design motif throughout India. Also known as *chopat* and *saktapar.*

chay — The plant (*Oldenlandia umbellata*) whose root is used for red dye on the eastern coast of India.

chir bhat — Gujarati double ikat *patola* with plain fields.

choli — A blouse worn by women with a sari or *ghaghara.*

dasphulia — Ten-flowered; indicates ten stripes of additional warp patterning along either selvedge in saris from Sambalpur district, Orissa.

dhoti — A man's draped and unstitched lower garment.

domuha — "Two-faces." An Orissan sari with a double *pallu.*

Ganesha Sthapana — *Sthapana* "to install a diety." In western India, a small household textile depicting the image of Ganesha, the elephant-headed god. The bridal couple first makes an offering to Ganesha to insure good fortune.

ghaghara — An ankle-length skirt gathered at the waist or made of sewn gored panels. It is the traditional dress of Rajasthani and Gujarati women and is worn with a *choli* and *odhani.*

gharchola — A *bandhana* wedding sari of Gujarat.

Gitagovinda — A Sanskrit poem written by Jayadeva of Orissa near the close of the twelfth century. The subject is the estrangement and reunion of Radha and Krishna.

haldi — Turmeric, used as a yellow dye.

haveli — From Persian, a surrounded or enclosed space; a large town house used as a place of worship by the Vallabhacharya sect of Nathadwara, Rajasthan.

jagri — Brown palm sugar often used in the preparation of dyes in both western and eastern India. See *kasam.*

kalam — Literally, "pen." A tool for applying mordants or wax to fabric.

kalamkari — Literally, "penwork." *Kalamkari* combines a series of processes including the application of mordant by *kalam* or block, immersion dyeing in red, resisting with wax, indigo dyeing, and direct application of dyes.

kambla — Literally, "blanket." A wrap for the shoulders worn by men in Gujarat. Also *dhabla.*

kamri — A man's tailored jacket.

kanat — One of a series of tent hangings or cloth screens placed around a courtly encampment.

kanguri — A niched battlement of a castle; an ornamental cornice; turret.

kasam — A fermented solution of *jagri* (brown palm sugar) and iron filings which produces a permanent black when applied to cloth treated in tannin.

khandua — An Orissan marriage *odhani.*

kumbha — Temple motif of Orissa.

laheriya — Literally, "wavy lines." Design name for bound resist turbans of Rajasthan.

Lakshmi Puja — The worship of Lakshmi, the goddess of good fortune.

lodha chhal — The bark of the tree *Symploco racemoze* which is used for red dye and for medicinal purposes.

lungi — A man's lower draped garment.

Mata Pachedi — A temple cloth of Gujarat for the Mother Goddess.

muktajhari — "Shower of pearls" design in Orissan textiles.

myrobalam — The dried astringent fruit of any of several Indian trees of the genus *Terminalia.* The fruit contains tannin which is often used as a premordant and which reacts with soluble iron salts to produce a fast black.

nari, kunjar, popat, phul bhat — A design in the Gujarati *patola* which consists of girls, elephants, parrots, and flowers enclosed in an overall diagonal gridwork of *chauks.*

nathva — A hand reel or pirn.

odhani, odhni, orhni — A woman's rectangular head covering traditionally worn in northern and western India.

padma — Lotus.

pagri — A turban.

pallavi, palla — The hem, border, or extreme end of a garment.

pallu — The decorative end of a sari.

pan bhat — The leaf design in Gujarati double ikat *patola.*

parda — Literally, "curtain."

patolu — A double ikat sari of Gujarat. (*Patola, pl.)*

phul bhat — The field of flowers design in Gujarati *patola.*

pichhavai — From *pichha,* "the back part or rear." A hanging for the Vaishnava temple of the Vallabhacharya sect, usually depicting scenes or ceremonies associated with the life of Krishna.

ratan chauk bhat — The jeweled diamond design in Gujarati *patola* derived from the *chauk.*

rumal — Literally, "handkerchief." A small square cloth that may be decorated by painting, printing, ikat or embroidery. See *telia rumal.*

saktapar — The *chauper* game board design used in saris from Sambalpur district, Orissa.

salwar — Trousers that are cut loose at the waist but are drawn tightly at the ankles.

sari — A woman's unstitched, draped garment, generally five to five-and-a-half yards long and the width of the loom, 45-48 inches.

saranguy — A tree (*Morinda citrifolia*) from which the leaves or roots were used to produce a red dye.

satrangi — Literally, "seven colors." A *laheriya* turban dyed with seven colors.

shloka — A stanza, couplet, or hymn of praise.

Simanta — A ritual performed in the seventh or eighth month of a woman's pregnancy; the parting of the locks of hair on the head in combing.

tasar — Wild silk from the *Antherala mylitta* and *paphia.*

telia rumal — A square ikat cloth from Andhra Pradesh used as a man's lower garment or turban. *Tel* (oil) was used in the dye process.

Vohra gaji bhat — A design of Gujarati *patola* made for the Bohra Muslims which contains a mixing of common *patola* motifs such as the *pan* leaf with the introduction of the caterpillar-like motifs distinct to this design.

Selected Bibliography

General

Anthropological Survey of India. *Peasant Life in India: A Study in Indian Unity and Diversity*. Calcutta: Indian Museum, 1961.

Chattopadhyay, Kamaladevi. *Handicrafts of India*. New Delhi: Indian Council for Cultural Relations, 1975.

Ciba Review: Batiks 58(July 1947).

———: *Ikats* 44(August 1942).

———: *Plangi Tie and Dye Work* 104(June 1954).

Irwin, John, and Margaret Hall. *Indian Painted and Printed Fabrics*. Ahmedabad: Calico Museum of Textiles, 1971.

———, and Margaret Hall. *Indian Embroideries*. Ahmedabad: Calico Museum of Textiles, 1973.

Jayakar, Pupul. *The Earthen Drum: An Introduction to the Ritual Arts of Rural India*. New Delhi: National Museum, 1980.

Kramrisch, Stella. *Unknown India: Ritual Art in Tribe and Village*. Philadelphia: Philadelphia Museum of Art, 1968.

Krishna, Vijay. "Flowers in Indian Textile Designs." *Journal of Indian Textile History*, no. 6. Ahmedabad: Calico Museum of Textiles, 1967: pp. 1-19.

Larsen, Jack Lenor, with Alfred Bühler, Bronwen and Garrett Solyom. *The Dyer's Art: Ikat, Batik, Plangi*. New York: Van Nostrand Reinhold, 1976.

Sreenivasam, Elsa. "Dye and Print Processes of India." *Surface Design Journal*, vol. 5 no. 4 (Summer 1981).

———. "Laheria, Bandhani and Kalamkari in India." *Surface Design Journal*, vol. 6 no. 2 (Winter 1981).

Watts, George, and Percy Brown. *Arts and Crafts of India*. New Delhi: Cosmo Publications, 1979. (First published as *Indian Art at Delhi*, 1903).

Orissa

Eschmann, Anncharlott, Herman Kulke, and Gaya Charan Tripathi. *The Cult of Jagannath and the Regional Tradition of Orissa*. New Delhi: Manohar, 1978.

Fischer, Eberhard, and Dinanath Pathy. "Textilien: Zeremonialstoffe," trans. by Edeltraud Harzer. In *Orissa: Kunst und Kultur in Nordost-Indien*. Zurich: Museum Reitberg, 1980.

Huyler, Stephen. "Folk Art in India Today." In *The Arts of India*, edited by Basil Gray. Oxford: Phaidon, 1981.

Mehta, R. N. "Bāndhas of Orissa." *Journal of Indian Textile History*, no. 6. Ahmedabad: Calico Museum of Textiles, 1961, pp. 62-74.

Miller, Barbara Stoler, trans. *Love Song of the Dark Lord: Jayadeva's "Gitagovinda."* New York: Columbia University Press, 1977.

Mohanty, Bijoy Chandra. *Applique Craft of Orissa*. Ahmedabad: Calico Museum of Textiles, 1980.

———, and Kalyan Krishna. *Ikat Fabrics of Orissa and Andhra Pradesh*. Ahmedabad: Calico Museum of Textiles, 1974.

Mishra, K. C. *Cult of Jagannath*. Calcutta: Firma K. L. Mukhopadhyay, 1971.

Oliver, Paul, ed. *Shelter, Sign and Symbol: An Explorative Work on Vernacular Architecture*. Woodstock, N.Y.: The Overlook Press, 1975.

Andhra Pradesh

All India Handicrafts Board. *Indian Kalamkari*. New Delhi: Government of India, Ministry of Industry, 1978.

Census of India. *Selected Crafts of Andhra Pradesh*, vol. 2, pt. 7-A(1). Delhi: Government of India, 1961.

Dalmia, Yasodhara. "Kalamkari: Transformation by Nelly Sethna." *MARG* 31, no. 4 (September 1978): pp. 81-85.

Jayakar, Pupal. "A Neglected Group of Indian Ikat Fabrics." *Journal of Indian Textile History*, no. 1. Ahmedabad: Calico Museum of Textiles, 1955, pp. 55-65.

Lintault, M. Joan. "Fabric Painting in India, the Kalamkaris of J. Gurappa Chetty." *Fiberarts* (Jan./Feb. 1982).

Mittal, Jagdish. "Telia Rumals of Pochampalli and Chirala." *MARG* 15, no. 4 (September 1962): pp. 26-29.

Rajasthan

Cousin, Francoise. "Lumiere et ombre, bleu et rouge: les *azrak* du Sind." *Objects et Mondes: La Revue du Musee de l'Homme*, 16, no. 2, (Summer 1976):pp. 65-78.

Sharma, G. N. *Social Life in Medieval Rajasthan*. Agra: Lakshmi Narain Agarwal Educational Publishers, 1968.

Skelton, Robert. *Rajasthani Temple Hangings of the Krishna Cult*. New York: The American Federation of Arts, 1973.

Talwar, Kay, and Kalyan Krishna. *Indian Pigment Paintings on Cloth*. Ahmedabad: Calico Museum of Textiles, 1979.

Yacopino, Felicia. *Threadlines Pakistan*. Karachi, Pakistan: Ministries of Industries, Government of Pakistan, 1977.

Gujarat

Bühler, Alfred, and Eberhard Fischer. *The Patola of Gujarat*, 2 vols. Basle, Switzerland: Museum of Ethnography, 1979.

Census of India. *Selected Crafts of Gujarat: Bandhani or Tie and Dye of Jamnagar*, vol. 5, pt. 7-A. Delhi: Government of India, 1961.

DeBone, Mary Golden. "Patolu and Its Techniques." *Textile Museum Journal* 4, no. 3 (1976):pp 49-62.

E son, Vickie C. *Dowries from Kutch: A Women's Folk Art Tradition in India*. Los Angeles: Museum of Cultural History, University of California, 1979.

Erikson, Joan. *Mata ni Pachedi: A Book on the Temple Cloth of the Mother Goddess*. Ahmedabad: National Institute of Design, 1968.

Fischer, Eberhard, Jyotindra Jain, and Haku Shah. "Mātāno Candarvo: Textile Pieces for Goddess Worship in Gujarat." In *MARG* 31, no. 4, (September 1978):pp. 61-63.

———, and Haku Shah. *Rural Craftsmen and Their Work: Equipment and Techniques in the Mer Village of Ratadi in Saurashtra, India*. Ahmedabad: National Institute of Design, 1970.

Frater, Judy. "The Meaning of Folk Art in Rabari Life: A Closer Look at Mirrored Embroidery." *Textile Museum Journal* 4, no. 2(1975): pp. 47-60.

Gillion, Kenneth L. *Ahmedabad: A Study in Indian Urban History*. Berkeley: University of California Press, 1968.

Nanavati, J. M., M. P. Vora, and M. A. Dhaky. *The Embroidery and Bead Work of Kutch and Saurashtra*. Ahmedabad: Department of Archaeology, 1966.